Dream, Phantasy and Art

The New Library of Psychoanalysis was launched in 1987 in association with the Institute of Psycho-Analysis, London. Its purpose is to facilitate a greater and more widespread appreciation of what psychoanalysis is really about and to provide a forum for increasing mutual understanding between psychoanalysts and those working in other disciplines such as history, linguistics, literature, medicine, philosophy, psychology, and the social sciences. It is intended that the titles selected for publication in the series should deepen and develop psychoanalytic thinking and technique, contribute to psychoanalysis from outside, or contribute to other disciplines from a psychoanalytical perspective.

The Institute, together with the British Psycho-Analytical Society, runs a low-fee psychoanalytic clinic, organizes lectures and scientific events concerned with psychoanalysis, publishes the *International Journal of Psycho-Analysis* and the *International Review of Psycho-Analysis*, and runs the only training course in the UK in psychoanalysis leading to membership of the International Psychoanalytical Association – the body which preserves internationally agreed standards of training, of professional entry, and of professional ethics and practice for psychoanalysis as initiated and developed by Sigmund Freud. Distinguished members of the Institute have included Michael Balint, Wilfred Bion, Ronald Fairbairn, Anna Freud, Ernest Jones, Melanie Klein, John Rickman, and Donald Winnicott.

Volumes 1–11 in the series have been prepared under the general editorship of David Tuckett, with Ronald Britton and Eglé Laufer as associate editors. Subsequent volumes are under the general editorship of Elizabeth Bott Spillius, with Christopher Bollas, Juliet Mitchell-Rossdale and Rosine Jozef Perelberg as associate editors.

IN THE SAME SERIES

NEW LIBRARY OF PSYCHOANALYSIS
—— 12 ——
General editor: Elizabeth Bott Spillius

Dream, Phantasy and Art

HANNA SEGAL

TAVISTOCK/ROUTLEDGE
LONDON AND NEW YORK

First published in 1991
by Routledge
11 New Fetter Lane, London EC4P 4EE

Simultaneously published in the USA and Canada
by Routledge
a division of Routledge, Chapman and Hall Inc.
29 West 35th Street, New York, NY 10001

Typeset by LaserScript Limited, Mitcham, Surrey
Printed in Great Britain by Mackays of Chatham

British Library Cataloguing in Publication Data

Segal, Hanna, *1918–*
Dream, phantasy and art. – (New Library of Psychoanalysis).
1. Psychological aspects
I. Title II. Series
700.19

Library of Congress Cataloging in Publication Data

Segal, Hanna.
Dream, phantasy and art / Hanna Segal.
p.   cm. — (New library of psychoanalysis : 12)
Includes bibliographical references.
1. Dreams.   2. Fantasy.   3. Psychoanalysis and art.   I. Title.
II. Series.
BF1078.S375   1991   90–33150
154.6'3—dc20   CIP

ISBN 0-415-01797-1
0-415-01798-X (pbk)

For Gabriel

Contents

Foreword

BETTY JOSEPH

All writing must to some extent reflect the personality of its author, and this book is no exception. It reflects the breadth of Hanna Segal's interests and her capacity to follow and explore their nature, and yet it is based in a strict theoretical framework, which she herself has extended and applied. Throughout her work, and indeed her living, one can see the interconnecting of these elements, her ability to extend boundaries and enjoy it.

She was born in Poland in 1918. Her mother was a woman of character and stamina, and a beauty. Her father was a man of wide interests; when aged twenty, while studying law in Paris, he wrote a history of French sculpture in the nineteenth century, which is still considered a classic in Poland. He was a barrister in Warsaw, but in the early thirties emigrated to become editor of an international newspaper in Geneva. Hanna Segal was twelve when the family left Poland, but she had and has always remained deeply attached to her roots there, and, at sixteen, she persuaded her parents to let her go back to Poland, where she finished school and studied medicine. The war found her in Paris, where her parents were, and when Paris was occupied by the Nazis, following the usual war trek, she arrived in London, and went on to Edinburgh, where she resumed her studies.

She was widely read in Freud and, while in Edinburgh she discovered the work of Anna Freud and Melanie Klein, and made up her mind to train with Klein. She was fortunate in finding in Edinburgh Dr David Matthews, who had himself been analysed by Klein, and he offered to take her into analysis while she was waiting to return to London. She came to London, was accepted for training by the British Psycho-Analytical Society and for analysis by Melanie Klein, qualifying in 1945. It was soon after this that we first met, so that our friendship has extended over more than forty years. By the time she was thirty-two, she was a Training Analyst.

These various elements emerge and are reflected in this book; the firm logical approach of the scientist, the love of beauty and desire to explore it, the search for the truth within as well as without, and the breadth of the explorer whose world must be boundless. This is important, because this book does not aim just to apply psychoanalysis to other areas – say, art and play – but the various interests grow from and enrich one another. This aspect, I think, was well expressed by Robert Langs in his introduction to her book of collected papers, published in 1981, *The Work of Hanna Segal; a Kleinian Approach to Clinical Practice: Delusion and Artistic Creativity and Other Psycho-Analytic Essays*. Speaking of certain papers in that book, he described them as standing not so much as 'essays in applied psycho-analysis, as integral elaboration of her clinical theoretical perspective'. Perhaps it is the richness of the interests and the depth of the thinking within the clinical theoretical perspective that gives this book both its sense of essential logic and its sense of freshness and creativity. Of course, there is a risk when boundaries are crossed in this way, it lays the writer open to criticism from writers in other fields, but Hanna Segal is willing to take that risk.

The logic of this book seems very clear; at the beginning, Hanna Segal introduces the reader to Freud's theory of dreams and brings her own clinical examples. This impels her to pause and talk about one of the main facets of dreams and dreaming – unconscious phantasy, which in Klein's view is basic to all mental and emotional activity. Here she moves freely between Freud's and Melanie Klein's ideas, relating phantasy not only to dreams, but also to Freud's thinking on the movement from the pleasure principle to the reality principle, which she links with Klein's ideas on the movement from the paranoid-schizoid position towards the depressive position.

Segal thus sees the discussion on phantasy as essential to our understanding of dreams, but incomplete without more thought on symbolism, an area in which she made a particularly original and important contribution as far back as 1957. In the chapter on symbolism she takes the reader through the ideas that Freud put forward, elaborated by Jones, and on to Klein's ideas and her own continuation of Klein's thinking, which she extends and elaborates. She differentiates between what she calls the symbolic equation and symbolism proper, showing how the former is based on functioning within the paranoid-schizoid position, particularly the powerful use of projective identification. She clarifies the difference between the symbolic equation and genuine symbol formation, which she shows can only take place within the depressive position. In her chapter on 'Mental Space and Elements of Symbolism', Segal links this work in some detail with Bion's theory of thinking. The reasoning in this section, while very fresh, is more difficult, but the vividness of the case material helps the reader to digest the meaning. It opens up a greater understanding of the problems of the ego that cannot dream in the ordinary sense of the word.

The chapter on 'The Dream and the Ego' is devoted to pathological aspects of dreaming, in which concrete aspects can be seen to predominate. She describes dreams which appear to serve the purpose in analysis, not primarily of communication, but acting in, or evacuation; dreams which she calls predictive; dreams where the important element to be analysed is not so much the content, but the way of telling them or behaving in relation to them. It is here that the previous chapters on phantasy and symbolic thought come clearly together with the dream topic; the partially or completely failed dream-work can be seen to be linked with poor symbol formation and concrete thinking.

In 1947 Hanna Segal read her first paper to the British Psycho-Analytical Society, 'A Psycho-analytic Approach to Aesthetics', which was published in 1952. This paper had a very important influence not only on analysts, but also on many people with little or no knowledge of psychoanalysis, but engaged in creative work themselves. It clearly touched something very important in their understanding. In the present book, she returns to this interest, which has always been with her, and about which she had written a number of papers in the intervening years. She goes back to Freud and to his contribution to the understanding of art and artists, as well as the criticisms that have been made of his approach. She opens up the issue of the relation between art, dreaming and day-dreaming, which she is now able to take further through her work on symbolism. She discusses, in a way both fresh and compelling, the relation between real art and the artist's capacity to face and deal with pain, ugliness and death – art and the depressive position. She takes the discussion back full circle, to the relation to a sense of reality; a relationship which she believes has to be highly developed in the artist, in contrast to the work of the day-dreamer and the 'failed' artist. And from here she sets out logically again into a consideration of similarities, differences and interconnections between day-dreaming, play, art, and creative thinking.

I have tried to indicate something of the movement and the inherent logic of this book, rooted in clinical experience, which not only illustrates, but is the base from which her theoretical discussions emerge. It is thus not a theoretical book, nor clinical, nor applied. The different aspects are essentially interconnected, which is indeed one of the things that makes Hanna Segal not only a very considerable thinker and writer but also a much sought-after teacher. Her writing and her lecturing have done much to enrich psychoanalysis and Melanie Klein's contribution to it, and also to make it available to a larger public, not only because of her clarity and stimulating intelligence, but also because of the depth and breadth of her concerns.

Betty Joseph 1990

Acknowledgements

My gratitude and thanks are due to the following: to my patients, whose work in their analyses enabled mine; to my husband, as always, for his unfailing support and for his helpful criticism; to Betty Joseph and Elizabeth Spillius, who read the whole manuscript, in the case of some chapters, several drafts, and whose comments were invaluable; to Riccardo Steiner for help with the first two chapters and for acquainting me with the significance of some of Freud's formulations in German, which were not fully conveyed in the English translation; to Richard Holmes for permission to quote from his book *Footsteps*; and finally to Ann Jameson and her computer who between them gave me excellent secretarial services, and compiled and checked the references; and to Albert Dickson for compiling the index.

Introduction

When in my adolescence I first read Freud it was very exciting to discover that psychoanalysis addressed itself to all fields of human endeavour and could throw a light on pathology and achievement alike, and that the practice of psychoanalysis could satisfy equally a wish for a therapeutic endeavour in psychoanalytic practice and an interest in the humanities.

At the beginning of my practice I was lucky in having among my patients both some artists and some psychotics. Both those kinds of patient draw one's attention to the crucial importance of symbolism and its vicissitudes. Psychoanalysis, I discovered, and rediscovered again and again, is a unique tool for investigating it.

Since that time I have written a number of papers on the subject of phantasy, dream, symbolism, and art. I have also lectured on these subjects in various settings to various audiences and on various levels. The editors of this series thought that it would be worth while for me to try and bring together my thoughts on those themes. I am grateful to them for stimulating me to attempt to do so in this book. The way I conceived this book dictated the way I deal here with references to other authors. I try to show the development of my thought without discussing other views or entering into controversies. I include only those works which illuminated my problems at the time I was struggling with them. Thus, for instance, in the chapter on art I quote extensively from Rodin and other artists. But of art critics and writers on aesthetics I refer only to Bell and Fry because I found their views on aesthetics illuminating and some of their criticism of psychoanalytic writers in the field relevant. Of psychoanalytic writers, my main inspiration comes of course from Freud and Klein. Later, Bion added considerably to my own understanding of symbolism and thought processes. These apart, I refer to only a few authors who influenced me at various times. A technical problem preoccupied me: how to make my writing interesting enough for psychoanalysts and yet accessible to the more general reader. Chapters 1 to 5 start easily with Freud's and Klein's basic ideas, and become increasingly complex as I go deeper and into more detail into psychotic processes in symbolization and thinking. Chapters 6 and 7 about art, and 8 about day-dream, imagination, and play, will again be more easily accessible to the general reader, though I hope not without interest to psychoanalysts.

This is not a book on technique, though some comments about technique are unavoidable. But when in the text I give an 'interpretation' of dreams it is not necessarily what I actually told the patient at the time. I use the dream to illustrate the mental processes I describe and my understanding of them. A few times I quote the actual interpretations given in the session because certain processes can be illustrated only by the actual interplay between analyst and patient.

1

The royal road

In the *New Introductory Lectures* Freud says of his theory of dreams:

> It occupies a special place in the history of psycho-analysis and marks the turning point; it was with it that analysis took the step from being a psychotherapeutic procedure to being a depth-psychology.
> (Freud, 1933: 7)

This is not surprising. Freud's studies of neuroses revealed to him the significance and psychic meaning of symptoms. It is the study of dreams – a universal phenomenon – which opened up the understanding of the universal domain of dream thought and dream language which goes far beyond the understanding of the actual night dream. Freud came to see the analysis of dreams as the royal road to the unconscious.

Unlike many of his other theories, Freud altered but little his theory of dreams, first fully formulated in *The Interpretation of Dreams* (1900), the book which, according to Jones, he considered his most important work.

Freud regards dreams as guardians of sleep. As we know, sleep can be disturbed by external stimuli such as a loud noise. To protect sleep, the sleeper can produce a dream in which the noise is taken up by the dream and, as it were, explained away. These are rare occasions. More regularly our sleep is disturbed by internal stimuli. Unfulfilled desires and wishes, unresolved conflicts, give rise to inner tensions which could trouble our sleep. In sleep our relation to reality is temporarily suspended. Repression is partly relaxed and regression occurs so that archaic unconscious wishes strive for expression. Motility and action are suspended and repressed desires seek expression 'in a harmless hallucinatory experience' (Freud 1933: 16). Common speech recognizes the wish-fulfilling aspect of dreams by using the same term 'dream' both for the day-dream (a wish-fulfilment fantasy) and the dream we have whilst asleep. But there is a fundamental difference between the two. The day-dream expresses conscious wishes –

3

organized, rationalized, acceptable to our waking consciousness. In the night dream, on the contrary, it is precisely those wishes which have been repressed and which trouble our psychic life that seek fulfilment. Freud thought at that time that dreams are predominately (though contrary to the common belief never exclusively) of a sexual nature. St Augustine, in his confessions, complains bitterly that God should permit that he be troubled by sexual dreams. He says that it would be so easy for God to arrange it differently. Had St Augustine been familiar with psychoanalysis, he would know that the task is not so simple. One cannot overestimate the importance of repressed sexuality in dreams, though originally Freud may have underestimated the equal importance of repressed aggression. Wishes which are powerful enough and dynamic enough and yet repressed enough to call for an expression in the dream rather than in reality invariably have their roots in infantile conflicts repressed in childhood but continually active in the unconscious. 'Dreaming is a piece of infantile mental life that has been superseded' (Freud 1900). Only infantile wishes have the power to mobilize forces which produce the dream:

> These wishes in our unconscious, ever on the alert and so to say immortal, remain one of the legendary Titans, weighed down since primeval ages by the massive bulk of the mountains which were once hurled upon them by the victorious gods and which are still shaken from time to time by the convulsion of their limbs.
>
> (Freud 1900: 553)

The dream is usually linked with some event which happened in daytime. Freud called this event a 'day residue'. Such an event may be important enough to make it understandable that it should influence the dream. But whether important or trivial, the day residue is an event which in some way is in the patient's mind connected with and represents some deeper unconscious conflict. In some way the day residue which triggers off the dream is similar to an event which could have triggered off the onset of a neurosis or of a particular neurotic symptom. Non-fulfilment of deep-seated wishes gives rise to inner tensions. Their fulfilment, however, would give rise to anxiety and guilt. It is not for nothing that these wishes were repressed in the first place. Freud's basic work on dreams precedes his concept of the superego. He calls the repressing agency that forbids the fulfilment of wishes unacceptable to consciousness, the censor, or the censorship, and he describes the conflict as between the unconscious wishes striving for expression and wish-fulfilment in the dream and the censorship which forbids such fulfilment. The ego does not disappear in sleep. It must protect itself both from the tension arising out of

4

unfulfilled desires and the anxiety and guilt that would accompany their fulfilment. Freud sees dreams as the result of a compromise between the repressed and the repressing forces – a way of bypassing the dream censorship.

A dream is produced by what Freud calls dream-work. The dream-work converts the latent dream thoughts unacceptable to the ego even in the state of sleep into the apparently innocuous manifest dream content. The dream-work is Freud's first description of a wider concept which is, I think, fundamental to the understanding of psychoanalysis, that is, psychic work.

Psychic dream-work aims at fulfilling the unacceptable and conflicting wishes by disguising them, and it evolves a particular mode of expression – the dream language. This is constructed by such mechanisms as condensation, displacement, indirect representation of various kinds, and symbolism. Those mechanisms Freud calls sometimes 'agents', sometimes 'Werkmeisters' (foremen, or masters), again conveying the psychic powers that create a dream.

Displacement can be of two kinds. One is the displacement of psychic values. The manifest dream may put emphasis on a dramatic and apparently important situation, but it is some insignificant detail that contains the most important latent dream thought. For instance, a patient, through a concatenation of circumstances, had a glimpse into a room in my house and he saw a print which he thought was of Venice. That night he had a long dream in which *he was walking with a girl in a place which reminded him of Venice*. That part of the dream led to a lot of associations, coming without much resistance, having to do with his past flirtations with girls, with fantasies about me and my holiday, and a fantasy of meeting me on holiday. But there was a detail in the dream to which he offered no spontaneous associations and which, in the dream, had no apparent emotional significance, compared with the richly evocative scene with the girl. There was somewhere in the background of his walk in the dream a concrete structure at the seaside. I asked him what this detail made him think of. Here the associations were much less pleasant. He said that he once saw at the Venice Lido remnants of German military installations. This in turn led him to associations about the German concentration camps and the extermination of Jews. That took him back to the glimpse he had of the room in which he saw the print and some books and he said that he had the thought that he 'was trapped in a Jewish household'. He connects Jewishness with intellectual and artistic interests; and his feelings about Jewishness are ambivalent. There was a great deal in him of unconscious anti-Semitism, which consciously is rather repugnant to him. It is the insignificant detail in the dream which contained all his

5

repressed hostility and cruel unconscious wishes, his, unacceptable to him, anti-Semitism, stimulated by the thought of my family life and the holiday he imagined me having. But in the dream it is displaced and condensed in a little detail and is ignored in associations; and there is a displacement of the importance to the more innocuous parts of the dream. He unconsciously wished that my husband and I would perish in a German concentration camp.

Another kind of displacement is the displacement of feelings or phantasies belonging to one situation on to another. A patient dreamed of *an angry quarrel with a man towards whom he had no antagonism, but in the background there was the figure of another man loosely connected by a similarity of name with the first one.* Towards that man he had many hostile thoughts, the expression of which would give rise to guilt, as he was much beholden to that man. An incomplete displacement of that kind is shown in the following dream.

A man dreamed that *he saw a little chicken being quartered, and he heard the desperate crying of a baby or a small child. After a while he realized that the sound was coming not from the chicken but from a small child who was nearby.* In this dream, the phantasied attack he had wished to make on his baby brother is displaced on to the chicken, but the displacement is not quite successful. It is a little boy who cries and the dreamer woke up in anguish.

This kind of displacement can also be seen as indirect representation: one man represents the other; the chicken represents a brother.

Condensation is an invariable feature of dreams. However short the dream, the latent thoughts that it contains range widely, and many thoughts and wishes, often contradictory ones, are contained in the dream as a whole and in the various elements of the dream. That is one of the reasons why it is difficult to report fully on the analysis of a dream, and indeed a dream can never be analysed fully in one session. In the next session the patient brings new associations and new dreams long before the analysis of the first one can be exhausted – if indeed it can ever be.

An interesting example of condensation has been shown to me in a repetition dream dreamed by Patient O, who suffered from a gastric ulcer. He has had this dream, close to a nightmare, on and off ever since he can remember. As a very small child he remembers waking up from his dream in a panic. In the dream *he is completely tied to a chair in a half-lying position. From all sides he is threatened by some elongated animals with crocodile mouths.*

In the course of his analysis the dream first occurred in the context of castration fears of having his penis bitten off or chopped off as a punishment for masturbating. He is being tied to a chair to immobilize his hands. It appeared again in the context of a phantasy of myself being pregnant, and anxiety about attacking the inside of my body and the babies therein. The unformed elongated shapes with crocodile mouths represented the dangerous babies inside mother. The dream kept recurring in various contexts. One day I was struck by his description of himself in the chair as being in a way bandaged to it, and that he himself was the elongated shape. I asked if he had ever been swaddled, and he told me that he was completely swaddled up to the age of three or four months. He also told me that he apparently suffered severely from abdominal colic (as it was diagnosed) at that time. It seemed to me then that the animals attacking him, the huge, angry, hungry mouths, were a projection of his own bodily perception of himself immobilized, hungry, and with a perception of his hungry mouth as enormous. Probably swaddling intensified the process of a violent projective identification of his perception of himself, as he was deprived of any kind of motor discharge by his musculature.

From the time of our work on that level, the dream stopped recurring. As the dream was formed it seems to have condensed his experiences at many different levels. In this condensation it also shows how the earliest primitive phantasies coloured, and found expression in, later phantasies and anxieties. My understanding of this dream derives, of course, not only from Freud's concept of condensation and displacement, but also from my own experience and from later theoretical developments. For instance, I used the concept of projective identification to understand the way unconscious phantasies were expressed in the dream, and I saw the condensation in this dream as an evolution from very primitive oral and concretely psychosomatic phantasy to a later, more symbolic level.

A more complex condensation is illustrated by a tiny fragment of a much longer dream. In the fragment the patient *saw the analyst accompanied by a little hairy boy or man who looked rather ridiculous and jumped around the analyst in a very subservient way.* His associations were to another analysand of mine who has a nice crop of dark hair and is not very tall. The patient had some reason to feel jealous of that man, who was professionally ahead of him. He had met the man the previous day and on that occasion felt rather contemptuous of him. This is the day residue. He remembered that he thought that my husband looked rather like a gorilla and his own father had a very hairy chest. He often meets in my street a long-haired adolescent whom he describes as 'rather a hood' and whom he thinks is my son. He met that boy also in the vicinity of the Tavistock Clinic and wondered if he was treated there. He thought I must be a very bad mother, neglecting my children so that they needed treatment. The subservient attitude he linked with himself, always coming punctually to the sessions and feeling abjectly dependent, which is a feeling he hates.

But the little man in the dream did not look quite human. The patient had recently seen a film about a werewolf. The figure in the dream could well be a werewolf.

So up to that point one could say that the figure in the dream represents a rival – my other analysand, my husband, and my son. They are all condensed into one figure. Past and present are equally condensed. My husband and son and his father and brother are all represented by one figure. But there are many other ideas represented in that fragment of a dream. The father and my husband, standing for him, are derided by being made small and ridiculous. There is also the fear of the rival, thus attacked – werewolves and gorillas are dangerous – but the fear is counteracted by his being made small and ridiculous. There is also the idea of my cruelty and badness, as accounting for the bad psychological state, not only of my supposed son, but of himself as my son. They both suffer from my neglect and I am blamed for their neuroses. Towards the end of the session there was a further association which revealed an even more painful repressed thought.

Whilst speaking of werewolves, he said, 'According to the legend, you become a werewolf if you are bitten by one. I suppose the wolf is at the door now.' He was referring to an impending holiday. So there is another layer to the dream. When the analyst, the feeding mother, goes away, he dreads hunger, felt like a biting wolf – the wolf is at the door. This bite of the wolf makes him into a werewolf. It mobilizes his oral greed and aggression, to which is added an extreme jealousy of those he thinks will stay with me – husband and son. In the dream he deals with his werewolf-like feelings by projecting them into his rivals, thus achieving the double aim of getting rid of pain and guilty feelings in himself and of attacking his rivals and making them bad. The resulting persecutory fear of his rivals now turned into werewolves is dealt with in a manic fashion by making the werewolf small and ridiculous. (He also projected into them his own smallness and the hated feeling of dependence, seen as subservient.) So one can see how one fragment of a whole long dream can condense and express a most complex psychical process.

What is the essence of what Freud so beautifully, I think, calls 'the dream thought'? I think Freud originally had in mind simply the repressed wish, disguised in the dream. But wishes are contradictory and complex, and I think the dream thought is more than a simple wish. It is itself a complex organization of wishes and defences. The dream thought of my patient's dream could be verbalized thus: 'When she goes away I am bitten by hunger. She is a bad biting figure inside my tummy. I feel full of greedy and biting feelings. This is intolerable. I shall put it into the rival who is with her. But that makes me frightened of the rival. I shall try to diminish and ridicule him', and so on. Condensation itself is not accidental. The dream thought, as I see it, is an expression of unconscious phantasy and our dream world is always with us.

In my understanding of condensation I may possibly differ from Freud. I do not think he sees condensation necessarily as a connected 'story'. He sees it more as various strands arising possibly from different impulses and trends of thought, converging together and being expressed in one condensed element.

Apart from condensation and displacement, there are other methods of transforming the latent dream thoughts; for instance, by indirect representation. There are many ways of achieving it: by similarity, the possession of a common attribute, using a part for a whole, by opposite, by verbal connection, and many, many others. Those representations, when understood, are sometimes very amusing – wit and humour, as Freud has shown, having similar features to the dream-work. As part of a long dream a patient dreamed *of a column of soldiers marching eight abreast.* Rather perplexed by that part of the dream, I asked her what she thought. She answered immediately: 'Ate a breast, of course. What else could it mean?'

A more complex example of representation by the opposite, or reversal, is shown in the dream of Patient B, with a manic character structure. The patient's mother died in his early adolescence and he avoided the mourning by schizoid and manic defences which deeply affected his character structure. The day preceding the dream, we were talking about a quite serious car accident he had had over the break and his preference for big and powerful cars over small cars, which his wife prefers, and in which he feels too vulnerable. He would really prefer to travel in armoured cars or tanks, he feels so vulnerable.

The next day I accidentally collected him from the waiting room a couple of minutes early. He said he was very pleased and felt warmly welcomed. After a time he reluctantly admitted that his first thought was very anxious: he thought I might have left the session with the previous patient early because I was ill, and it immediately reminded him of an operation I had had several years previously, and of his mother's unsuccessful breast-cancer operation.

He then told me a dream. *He was in a kind of lab. There were some chemical benches. Near him was a younger man, Bob. He slipped a little box into Bob's locker. Then a beautiful young woman brings the prize of £500, probably a winning in a raffle – 'when your number comes up you win'. She approaches him and Bob, and up to the last minute they do not know which of*

9

them is the winner and they both feel teased. Then she gives the prize to Bob.
He does not feel jealous; he feels generous, very much aware of how rich he is
and how poor Bob is. Bob is not only poor; he is also unworldly and naïve. He
would like, with the prize money, to buy a bottle of whisky for his wife, and
he turns to the patient to ask him if he can do that, and how one proceeds to do
it. The patient helpfully instructs him.

The patient's first batch of associations started with telling me that
Bob in the dream reminded him both of his brother and his eldest son
(his attitude to Bob reflects very much his attitude to his younger
brother) both as a child and as a young man, since his brother was
idealistic and became a poor parson, while the patient made mints of
money. The dream reminded him of all the ways in which he looked
after his brother as a small child, particularly after his mother's death,
but also later in life, when the patient administered the family estate.
The willingness with which he gave the prize made him think of his
elder son giving a family party now and he, the patient, in such a
situation feeling that he is giving way as paterfamilias.

The sum of £500 he did not link with anything. I made the
comment that everybody in the dream was younger than himself, but
he reminded me that a young woman could well stand for his mother
since his mother died young. And this led him to another batch of
associations. He remembered that his daughter, about whom he is
always troubled, is now approaching the age at which his mother died,
and it is also the time of the year close to the time his mother died. This
immediately drew my attention to the importance of reversal in the
dream. What he was concerned with was not his *lucky* number but his
unlucky number. His mother's number was up prematurely, it was
unlucky for him, and he has been recently preoccupied with his
vulnerability and his fear of death, stimulated by the car accident. Also
his son's growing up could be felt by him as his number coming up.

Once alerted to the importance of the reversal, we could see that
every element in the dream is reversed. The woman who gives the
prize is older than he (his mother), not younger; he feels not rich but
poverty-stricken, and this refers to two situations: first that his brother,
of whom he is acutely jealous, was born and got the prize from mother
(the little box) and later, when his mother died, he became an object
of special care and attention from his father. In the dream the patient
also feels generous and benevolent to his brother, which he would wish
to be, but in psychic reality he resented bitterly both the early care his
brother got from mother and the extra attention he got from father and
the family after mother's death, whilst my patient's needs were
completely ignored and he was expected to look after his brother. He
also at the time blamed his brother for her death, since some people

10

attributed her breast cancer to his little brother having bitten the breast when a baby.

After some bringing together of the underlying experience of the dream, represented in such a reversed fashion, he remembered that he did in fact inherit a little box from his mother but he did not give it to his brother. We then got an association to the £500. He had a bill for £500 for the urgent repairs to his car that had been smashed in the accident. He also remembered that for more than a week he forgot to pay my bill. So the dream has to do with urgent anxieties and needs of repair, and in contrast to the apparent generosity of the dream, a remaining reluctance to pay my bill, or the one for the repair of the car. So every element in the dream is reversed: the lucky number is the bad number; the benevolence and generosity replace rage and meanness. The jolly raffle is in fact a re-living of his mother's death and his fear for himself. Even the bottle of whisky in the dream is a kind of reversal. I made a comment at some point that Bob wanting to get a bottle of whisky for his wife, after getting the prize from the woman, could represent Bob's wanting to use the goodness he got from the breast in giving good sexuality to his wife. However, the patient immediately corrected me, since his association to cheap whisky was to a drunkard who committed incest with his daughter and committed suicide – very bad sexuality.

Right at the end of the session, he suddenly realized that the chemical lab with benches in his dream reminded him that, as his mother was dying of cancer, he used to spend hours in a little chemistry laboratory which he rigged up for himself cut off from the rest of the family and from his own feelings.

In this dream I think we can see how complex dream language is. One could say that in the dream everything is represented by its opposite, by the reverse, but at the same time that way of representing it changes a deeply traumatic situation into a wish-fulfilling one. One could look at the reversals of the dream as a disguise: an effect of dream language is to disguise a distressing experience, but at the same time in the dream language is hidden an unconscious wish to change the painful reality, internal and external, into a glorious raffle.

Each dreamer has a favourite style in his dream language and the style itself often reveals their personality. 'Le style c'est l'homme', said Buffon. It applies to dreams as well as to art. The very style of the dream, like the style of a personality, reflects the broad combination of object relationships, anxieties, and defences that moulds one's personality.

All the various methods of representing an idea in the dream constitute dream-work. Freud excludes symbols from dream-work. He

11

considered symbols as universal and deriving from the ancient past. He says:

> Things that are symbolically connected today were probably united in prehistoric times by conceptual and linguistic identity. They are, one could say, given, not achieved by psychic work implied in other methods of indirect representation.

(Freud 1900: 352)

This view of symbolism has been questioned implicitly by Melanie Klein and explicitly by myself, and I shall return to it later.

The process of analysing a dream is doing the dream-work in reverse. The associations to the dream expand again what had been condensed, rectify the displacement, decipher the indirect represent-ation. But the associations to the dream are not, as some therapists think, in themselves the latent content. They are only a path leading towards latent content, because repression continues to operate and to manifest itself as resistance. Indeed, it is from the clinical experience of resistance that Freud deduced the mechanism of repression (Heimann 1950) – a theoretical concept. The analysis of a dream proceeds against resistance. Trends of association break off or acquire a defensive character, or else the patient resists seeing the significance which may be apparent to the analyst. The interpretation of the analyst has to demonstrate the resistance and indicate the latent content. Where the patient's own work falters, the analyst's interpretation provides the missing link. The psychic work of deciphering the dream-work is essential in the analysis of dreams. This is done jointly by the patient and the analyst. It must be remembered that Freud did not say that dreams are the royal road to the unconscious. He said that the under-standing of dreams is the royal road to the unconscious, and this understanding has to be reached by psychic work.

There is a further factor which conceals dream thought and which operates after waking, and that is the distortion in the actual remem-bering of the dream whilst awake which Freud calls secondary elabor-ation. As we recollect, so we distort the dream. Sometimes in the session this more conscious distortion can be corrected and a more genuine remembrance of the dream emerges. This secondary elabor-ation, according to Freud, is a continuation of the repression of the latent dream thoughts. But he also describes how intolerable to our waking mind are illogicality, chaos, and disorder. He quotes Havelock Ellis:

> Sleeping consciousness we may even imagine as saying to itself in effect: 'Here comes our master, Waking Consciousness, who

12

attaches such mighty importance to reason and logic and so forth. Quick! gather things up, put them in order – any order will do – before he enters to take possession.'

(Freud 1900: 501)

Whether this need to rationalize and make sense, make a story, is not the same as resistance against latent unconscious dream thoughts I am not certain. It is also questionable what 'remembering' a dream is. After analysis of the secondary elaboration, one may recover a dream nearer to what was remembered immediately on waking. But in the course of the session new elements of the dream may appear. What is remembered may be altered as the dream reveals new aspects and deeper levels. The remembered dream has its roots, in my view, in an unconscious phantasy the full depth and extent of which can never be remembered.

Freud considered three kinds of dream. The first is the undisguised wish-fulfilment dream, characteristic of children. He reports a dream of a little girl in which she gorges on strawberries and of a little boy deprived of a meat dish dreaming of a 'roast that got itself eaten'. However, since we have learned to psychoanalyse children, I think we are much more doubtful about the innocence of such dreams. The second kind are dreams involving dream-work and disguised fulfilment of unconscious wishes, and it is to this kind of dream that the bulk of Freud's work is directed. The third kind are those dreams which seem to run counter to the wish-fulfilment theory: namely, anxiety dreams and punishment dreams. His comments before 1920 on those dreams are, first in relation to anxiety dreams, that the dreamer makes an attempt at fulfilling his wishes in a dream language but that this attempt is not necessarily successful. When an undisguised ego-dystonic wish breaks through, the ego will respond by anxiety. As to the punishment dreams, he reminds us that dreams are the outcome of various compromises between the censor and the instinctual desires, and in the punishment dreams it is the censor that has the upper hand.

Unlike his other theories, Freud never much altered his theory of dreams to bring it in line with the vast development of his theory of psychic life, particularly after 1920. Since *Beyond the Pleasure Principle* (1920) he saw the basic psychic conflict as that between the life and the death instinct. This was his final instinct theory. He then evolved the structural theory of mind – described in terms of the ego, the superego, and the id (Freud 1923). He had revised his theory of anxiety and repression (Freud 1926). Starting with the idea that anxiety was due to repression, he had come to realize that, on the contrary, it is anxiety which causes repression. This discovery was linked with his view that it is the ego, not the superego (the old 'censor'), that is responsible for repression as well as for a variety of other defence mechanisms. In the *New Introductory Lectures* (1933), in the chapter on 'The Revision of the Theory of Dreams' he did bring the theory partly up to date. For instance, he did bring in the superego in the place of the censor, and speaks of the dream having to reconcile the claims of the id and the superego. Since this was written after *The Ego and the Id* it would carry the implication that the superego contains the death instinct. But Freud does not explicitly bring the concept of the life and death instincts into the revision of his theory of dreams. He gives particular attention among anxiety dreams to the repetition in dreams of traumatic events which have led to a traumatic neurosis. And, like other anxiety dreams in which the wish-fulfilment role of dreams had failed, he explains the recurrent traumatic anxiety dream as being like other anxiety dreams – an example of the dream-work having failed in its wish-fulfilling task. However, by that time, in other publications (*Beyond the Pleasure Principle*, for instance) he speaks of those dreams as one of the important phenomena which made him develop his concept of the death instinct. But in his revision he does not seem to expand the idea that the work of the dream is not only to reconcile the forbidden wish and the superego or the ego, but also to find a compromise or resolution for contradictory unconscious wishes, and the basic conflict between the life and death instincts.

In the dream of Patient B, I emphasize his wish-fulfilment in converting the traumatic death of his mother into a happy, glorious event. However, that was not all there was to the dream. Why did he have that particular dream at that time? The context was that certain events had stirred in his transference a particular jealousy of a brother figure and brought about death wishes towards me and that represent-ative of his brother. His dream is a solution to his conflict between those death wishes and his reparative wishes in a wishful phantasy of bringing his mother back to life, helping his brother and giving him a prize, and so on, but without losing his sense of his great superiority to the latter.

Freud also evolved the concept of working through, but he did not explicitly apply it to the dream work as one of the ways of working through a conflict. He speaks of the dream as a harmless hallucination, a 'harmless dream-psychosis' (Freud 1933: 16). He also speaks of the dream as similar to psychosis but happening entirely in sleep. This seems to me in some way questionable, since the kind of psychic work elaborating a conflict, akin, I think, to a working through, which happens in the dream, is precisely what is lacking in psychosis. Freud says that anxiety dreams happen when the dream-work fails. Can we

14

today say more about this failure of the ego to perform the dream-work?

One is always struck by how formidable is the task of the ego in creating a dream. It has to carry out repression adequately, but not excessively. It has to be capable of the psychic work involved in dream-work, and I shall suggest that this includes the formation of symbols. What happens when the ego is too damaged to fulfil those functions? I think some of the later work done on the development of the ego and its pathology has thrown more light on these problems. I shall therefore return to dreams after discussing the concepts of unconscious phantasy and symbolism, and the differences between psychotic and non-psychotic functioning of the ego.

2

Phantasy

Freud's discovery of unconscious thoughts underlying hysterical symptoms can be seen as equivalent to the discovery of unconscious phantasy. He showed how conflicts, instincts, and defences are expressed and contained in an unconscious phantasy, such as, for instance the phantasy of fellatio in Dora's *globus hystericus*. Originally he thought of phantasies mainly as defences against memory: 'Phantasies are psychical façades constructed in order to bar the way to these memories' (Freud 1950 [1897]: *Letter to Fliess*). Having abandoned his seduction theory in favour of the view that seduction scenes which were apparently remembered or recovered from repression and believed to be fact were most frequently a child's wish-fulfilment phantasy, he gave phantasy a major place: 'Hysterical symptoms are not attached to actual memories but to phantasies erected on the basis of memories' (Freud 1900: 491).

In a letter to Fliess (21 September 1897), Freud says that his discovery made him realize that phantasies are as real and important as any external reality. After that he sometimes spoke of phantasy as *the* psychic reality (Freud 1914c: 18; 1925a: 34).

Unlike his theory of dreams, Freud never worked out in full a theory of unconscious phantasy. He never devoted a book, or even a paper, wholly to that subject, despite the importance of the concept in his work.

One could say that generally for Freud phantasy is pretty close to day-dreaming. It is a wish-fulfilling idea which comes into play when external reality is frustrating. Basically, a phantasy consists of an unconscious wish worked on by the capacity for logical thought so as to give rise to a disguised expression and imaginary fulfilment of the instinctual wish. Phantasies remain subordinate to the pleasure principle, but they are formed by the 'secondary process'; that is, by the normal rational logic that is characteristic of the Systems Preconscious and Conscious. Hence Freud sees phantasy as a rather late phenomenon, appearing

16

only when the reality principle and the capacity for logical thinking have been firmly established. In the case of conscious fantasies, day-dreams, the fantasy is known not to be true. When the wish-fulfilling fantasy is unacceptable to consciousness it is repressed and becomes unconscious phantasy. In his clearest statement about this, in the 'Formulations on the two principles of mental functioning' he says:

> With the introduction of the reality principle one mode of thought-activity was split off; it was kept free from reality-testing and remained subordinated to the pleasure principle alone. This activity is *phantasying*, which begins already in the children's play, and later, continued as *day-dreaming*, abandons dependence on real objects.
>
> (Freud 1911: 222)

If fantasies are found to be unacceptable to consciousness so that they are repressed into the System Unconscious, they are subject to the 'primary process', supremacy of the pleasure principle, no sense of time or temporal causation, and all the other features that Freud considered to be characteristic of the System Unconscious. Once they have been repressed into the System Unconscious, phantasies are no longer known to be untrue so that they become indistinguishable from memories. In the System Unconscious phantasies 'proliferate in the dark', as he put it.

Freud, however, seems uneasy about the exact relation between instinct and phantasy. On the one hand, phantasies were subordinate to the pleasure–pain principle, which implies they derive from instinct. On the other hand, he frequently states that at some point instincts attach themselves to phantasy. 'Every desire takes before long the form of picturing its own fulfilment' (Freud 1916–17: 372).

Freud's uncertainty about the exact relation between instinct and phantasy, and his prevalent view that they are a kind of repressed day-dream, may well be at the root of his hesitation about the role of phantasies in dreams.

In Chapter 6 of *Interpretation of Dreams* he writes:

> [I] cannot completely escape a consideration of phantasies in this connection since they often make their way complete into dreams and since still more often clear glimpses of them can be seen behind the dream.
>
> (Freud 1900: 493)

He says that phantasies that make their way into the dream are thereafter treated in general like any other portion of the latent material, though the phantasy often remains recognizable as an entity

17

in the dream. In describing those phantasies, he assumes that they must have undergone repression to appear in the dream. (At this point he seems to mean that they were conscious fantasies later repressed.) But he also speaks of primary phantasies which have never been conscious (which he directly connects with instincts).

> They strike me as being, as it were, more fluent, more connected, and at the same time more fleeting than other parts of the same dream. These, I know, are unconscious phantasies which find their way into the fabric of the dream, but I have never succeeded in pinning down a phantasy of this kind.
>
> (Freud 1900: 493)

He asks:

> Whence comes the need for these phantasies and the material for them? There can be no doubt that their sources lie in the instincts; but it has still to be explained why the same phantasies with the same content are created on every occasion.
>
> (Freud 1916-17: 370)

His answer is that they repeat 'what were once real occurrences in the primaeval times of the human family' (Freud 1916-17: 371).

It is in keeping with Freud's notion of phantasy being a relatively late phenomenon in mental life ('It begins with children's play') that he sees phantasies as highly organized and referring mainly to whole objects. More primitive phantasies do not enter much into his description. More primitive functioning on a pre-verbal, even pre-visual, psychosomatic level is not included in his concept of phantasy. Hence he does not connect early hallucinatory wish-fulfilment with phantasy, but only with memory.

Mostly Freud refers to unconscious phantasy as connected with pathology, but he is also very aware that it is only a 'short step' between phantasy resulting in a symptom or in artistic creativity; and in all his papers on works of art he views unconscious phantasy also as a source of sublimation. But seeing it as a kind of repressed day-dream, he cannot quite account for unconscious phantasy as a source of creative art and gets into difficulties in some of his theorizing about art. I shall return to this subject later.

It is as though Freud had opened a door to a fascinating, rich, mysterious world, but did not quite take the full measure of his own discovery and the connections between that and his other major discoveries, such as the dream-work and the dream language. It is the psychoanalysis of children which revealed the ubiquity and the dynamic power of unconscious phantasy, and Klein gave this concept its full weight. From the beginning of her work with children, she was struck by the extent to which the child's life is dominated by unconscious phantasy. In one of her earliest papers, 'The role of the school in libidinal development' (1923), she describes how all the child's activities, not only in play but also in work, contain an elaboration of unconscious sexual phantasies. At that time she was still mainly concerned with phantasies leading to neurotic symptoms like inhibitions in learning, such as her description of how a little girl could not learn grammar because parsing represented for her eating rabbit and that in turn was connected with unconscious cannibalistic phantasies; or the little boy who could not do division sums because it represented cutting his mother into bits; and so on. But in addition, one gets the impression of a rich unconscious phantasy life underlying the child's relation to school and all his activity: not just a pathological formation interfering with activities. In the consulting-room she observed the child's expression of his unconscious phantasies and realized the degree to which they could distort perception and dominate the child's life. And the younger the child, the more dominant was its unconscious phantasy life.

Most of Freud's statements give the impression that he thought of unconscious phantasies as if they were like islands in the sea of mental life. Reading Klein's work with children, one gets a glimpse of an internal phantasy world like a vast continent under the sea, the islands being its conscious, external, observable manifestations.

When it became apparent that her views on phantasy extended Freud's concept and in some way differed from his, Susan Isaacs addressed herself to this new use of the concept in her paper 'The nature and function of phantasy' (1948). As Freud had said, phantasies, like dreams, are wish fulfilments, but while he considered that they form relatively late in development, in Klein's and Isaacs' view they are active from the start. In the omnipotent mind of the infant and child desires become wish-fulfilling phantasies, and such phantasies are viewed by Klein and Isaacs as a direct expression of instincts and impulses. Unlike Freud, who considers, in some of his writings, that at some point instincts and phantasies get linked, Klein boldly assumes that instincts from the beginning of life give rise to phantasy. It is not at some point that 'every desire takes before long the form of picturing its own fulfilment' (Freud 1916–17: 372), but that such picturing is inherent in the process at all times.

Freud wavered between two definitions of instinct. In some papers he called it 'the psychical representative of the stimuli originating within the organism and reaching the mind' and 'the concept on the frontier between the somatic and the mental . . . the psychical representative of organic forces' (Strachey, in Freud 1915a: 112). In his later papers, however, he more often speaks of instinct itself as having a psychical representative. In 'The unconscious' he says:

> An instinct can never become an object of consciousness – only the idea that represents the instinct can. Even in the unconscious, moreover, an instinct cannot be represented otherwise than by an idea [which he also calls 'psychic representative'].
>
> (Freud 1915b: 177)

An instinct, according to Freud, has a source, an aim, and an object. The 'idea', which is the psychical representative of the instinct, in Klein's view includes a phantasy of a drive-fulfilling object.

The hallucinatory wish-fulfilment postulated by Freud would be seen by Klein and Isaacs as part of a primitive phantasy. Freud wondered, 'but it has still to be explained why the same phantasies with the same content are created on every occasion' (Freud 1916–17: 370). Taking the Klein and Isaacs view, the reason those phantasies are common to all humans is not that they reproduce some real events in the prehistoric past but that we share a common instinctual endowment and ways of dealing with it. All phantasy activity belongs to the ego, and some of the differences in views on phantasy mainly hinge on different views of the early ego. In Klein's view, from the beginning of life there is sufficient ego to experience anxiety, to form some object relationships in reality and phantasy, and to use primitive defences. Unlike Freud, she does not hold the view that phantasies can only be formed when the infant or child has developed a capacity for logical thought.

The view that phantasy is operative from the beginning, at the most primitive stages of development, implies that this phantasy is to begin with physical: the hallucinated breast is not to begin with a visual experience, but a bodily one. Early experiences, such as hunger or satisfaction, are experienced and interpreted by the infant in terms of object–relationship phantasies. Susan Isaacs assumes that behind every phantasy of introjection there is an earlier one of concrete incorporation. Satisfaction is experienced as containing a need-fulfilling object; hunger as a persecution. Our language reflects this. We speak of being 'gnawed by hunger'; or 'the wolf being at the door'. My favourite is the French: hunger being described as eating an enraged cow ('manger de la vache enragée'). Such primitive psychosomatic phantasies evolve with growth and reality-testing, but they remain at the core of our personality and can still play a dynamic part in later development. Physical experiences are interpreted as phantasy object relationships, giving them emotional meaning. A baby in pain may feel itself as being hated. But also, conversely, the phantasies are so close to the somatic that they affect physical functioning. It is well known that an emotionally upset baby often develops digestive and other physical symptoms. This may persist into adulthood, as in my Patient O [Chapter 1], whose unconscious phantasies resulted in a gastric ulcer.

After 1920, when Freud introduced the duality of the life and death instincts, he did not revise his views of the early hallucinatory wish-fulfilment; nor his views on primary narcissism. It is Klein who used the concept of the death instinct most fully in describing the functioning of the early ego. Thus in her view the early phantasy wish-fulfilments would relate not only to hallucinated or phantasied satisfaction of the libidinal wishes by an ideal object but would also relate to all those wishes springing from the death instinct. What Freud described as the deflection of the death instinct by the organism is seen by her as a projection by the ego of the death instinct into an object, giving rise to phantasies of an object which is destroyed and destructive (Segal 1964).

One can see here that from the start, in her view, phantasies have both a wish-fulfilling and a defensive aspect, since splitting and projection, which are mechanisms of defence, are also expressed through phantasies, just as are the impulses.

Phantasies of course are linked with defences. The very fact of phantasying is a defence against painful realities. Freud's earliest view was that phantasies were defences against memory, but it soon became apparent to him that they could be used as defences against any painful reality. However, though he recognizes that phantasies have a defensive function, he does not connect defence mechanisms with phantasies. Susan Isaacs firmly links the concept of phantasy with that of defences. According to her, the concept of defences is an abstract and generalized description of what the individual does actively in the particular content of his phantasies. Underlying the defences that we observe and describe in an abstract way is a detailed phantasy of their implementation.

I shall illustrate this with material from a little girl, aged two and a half, who suffered from severe sleeping and digestive difficulties. She presented what could be described as a splitting of the object into a good and bad figure in the following way.

She had missed her last session before the holidays because she had become ill with diarrhoea. In her first session after the holidays she became very much concerned with and frightened by a shapeless shadow on the wall, which she named 'the lady on the wall'. She started the session saying that she did not bring a cardigan because though it was cold outside it was so nice and warm in the room. And she smiled warmly at the analyst. But when she turned to the wall and saw the shadow she started screaming 'The lady on the wall! – it's nasty, it's bad! I don't like her! It bites! Put her into the dustbin!' She felt confronted by two objects in the room: the flesh-and-blood analyst felt as giving warmth and protection; and the lady on the wall full of threat. The analyst interpreted that the 'lady on the wall' was the bad analyst who was absent in the break; and the child relaxed and started looking at the wall in a questioning way. The analyst reminded her that the slight discoloration on the wall was due to the little girl having herself splashed it sometime before the holiday and reminded her of her diarrhoea, which deprived her of the session; and she linked it with her anger at the analyst and her wish to splash her with urine and fill her with faeces. This she believed turned the analyst in her mind into a bad lady like the lady on the wall. The child then relaxed more and started playing freely. She poured some water into a cup, called it 'milk for the baby' and produced a complicated game in which the baby was first refusing to take the milk, saying 'it's dirty', then shaking it and drinking it with great satisfaction.

This child, who had great feeding and sleeping difficulties as well as digestive troubles, was, I think, expressing positive and negative impulses as well as defences such as splitting and projection. In her anger at the break she fantasied that she put bad parts of herself (biting urine, faeces) into the analyst's breast, which then turned it into a very bad object. But she also loved and needed, and wished to keep in her mind, the good analyst. So she split off this badness from her image of the analyst and projected it on to the biting, dirty 'lady on the wall'. What in abstract terms was splitting, idealization, and projection was in the child's experience a vivid phantasy resulting in a near-hallucination.

The following material from an adult patient shows similarly the unconscious phantasies underlying the defence mechanism of splitting.

Here are two dreams described by a patient during the hour preceding my holiday.[1] In the first dream, *the patient was in a dark room which contained two human figures standing close to one another as well as other less well-defined people. The two figures were exactly alike, except that one of them looked drab and dark, while the other was illuminated. The patient was sure that she alone could see the illuminated figure – it was invisible to other people in the dream.*

The patient made extensive use of the mechanisms of splitting, denial, and idealization. She had had the opportunity that same week to see me in a room full of people, a situation unusual for her, and her association with the dream was that the two figures represented myself.

One was the person whom everybody could see in the crowded room, but the other one was 'her analyst', her special possession. She felt that she was not going to mind the holiday any more than she had minded or had been jealous about seeing me with other people, because she had this special relation to me which was permanently hers alone. In the first dream it is clear that she deals with her jealousy, stirred both by seeing me with other people and by the analytic holiday, through splitting and idealization; she has got the illuminated, idealized analyst whom no one can take away from her.

In the second dream the patient dreamed that *there was a small girl sitting on the floor cutting out paper with a pair of scissors. She was keeping the cut-out piece to herself; the floor was covered with discarded bits of paper which other children were busy collecting.*

The second dream is another fuller version of the first: it shows how this splitting and idealization were in fact felt by her. The splitting is expressed in the cutting. She is the little girl who has cut out of her analyst the cut-out figure which, like the illuminated figure in the first dream, is her analyst's good part. The people who could only see a drab analyst-figure are represented in the second dream by the children who have nothing but the discarded bits. The splitting seen in the first dream is clearly experienced in the second dream as an attack, an actual cutting of her analyst into an ideal part and a worthless part; and what is represented in the first dream as idealization is experienced in the second dream as taking and retaining for herself the best cut-out bits of her analyst. The second dream makes it clear that, for this patient, the processes of splitting and idealization were felt as a very aggressive, greedy, and guilty activity.

Phantasies can defend against realities, but they also defend against other phantasies. For instance, phantasies of an idealized object and an idealized self are both a wish-fulfilling phantasy and a defence against underlying terror.

A patient for a long time tenaciously maintained a very idealized and rigid relationship to me. But it was very brittle. Any disappointment, and particularly any hint of a possible narcissistic injury, would lead to the phantasy collapsing, and she would experience blackness and terror. Gradually we got in touch with the most horrifying phantasies of herself disintegrating, disappearing, and being subject to endless persecution. It became apparent that she had to maintain this idealization of me because of her conviction that neither she nor I would ever be able to stand the intensity of her hatred, terror, and despair.

Thus phantasies are a meeting-ground between impulses and defences, as in Freud's description of the dream as a compromise formation between impulses and defences. Klein, though, sees unconscious phantasy not so much as a compromise but as an expression of both impulses and defences.

'Unconscious phantasies form the operative link between instincts and mechanisms' (Isaacs 1948: 112).

However, there is a further important link to be made, and this is one between unconscious phantasy and the structure of the personality. If one thinks of Freud's structural model, the superego is a structure resulting from a phantasy of having introjected an object, and the nature of that object taken inside in phantasy is determined not only by the reality of the object but also by the projections of the child's impulses. And such a projection done in phantasy results in the creation of a phantasy internal object.

If phantasies exist from the beginning of life, early phantasies of projection and introjection would lay a base for the personality structure. Rosenfeld, in his paper on 'The psycho-analysis of the superego conflict in an acute schizophrenic patient' (1952) shows how in a session the patient demonstrated that he had a phantasy of three painful internal objects which could be called an early superego. They were the lupus, a brown cow, and a yellow cow. As was clear from this and the preceding sessions, the lupus was a punitive superego directed at the patient's oral sadism; the yellow cow was the superego for his urinary, envious, and jealous attacks and the brown cow in Rosenfeld's view was a destroyed breast changed into faeces. (I think it was, probably, similarly to the urinary yellow cow, also a breast filled with faeces by projection.)

The phantasies underlying a much more evolved superego are illustrated by the dream of a neurotic patient.[2] Presented by him very early in his analysis, the dream illustrates the relation between unconscious phantasy, reality, mechanisms of defence, and ego structure. The patient was an officer in the Polish navy. He had a very rigid personality. He often felt his superior officers as overbearing, but he also had a very strict inner sense of honour and duty by which he felt oppressed. He was afraid of being too strict with the sailors, with whose rebelliousness he often felt identified. They also presented him with great homosexual temptations and guilt, since as his own subordinates he considered them as the most forbidden objects. He dreamed *of a pyramid. At the bottom of this pyramid there was a crowd of rough sailors, bearing a heavy gold book on their heads. On this book stood a naval officer of the same rank as himself, and on his shoulders an admiral. The admiral, he said, seemed in his own way to exercise as great a pressure from above and to be as awe-inspiring as the crowd of sailors who formed the base of the pyramid and pressed up from below.*

24

I was of course rather suspicious of the dream as bookish. But I had gathered that the patient knew very little about psychoanalysis. Later on I found out that all he knew was that Freud and psychoanalysis had something to do with sex. In his associations he identified the admiral with his father, who in reality was rather rigid and oppressive, and the sailors with his own rebellious and sexual feelings. He also said that the admiral was just as strong and frightening in the dream as the sailors. He tried to keep to the 'golden mean' and felt squashed between the two.

This made it clear that the severity of his superego was also due to his own projections. We can see here the interrelation between phantasy and external reality, the reality of the father being altered by projections. His defence mechanism of repression is represented in the phantasy by the combined pressure of the admiral-superego and the officer-ego trying to keep the instincts, represented by the sailors, under. We can also see the operation of projection and introjection, in that his father is altered by projections since his power is the same as that of the sailors and he is introjected to form the superego.

The dream was such a clear pictorial representation of his mental structure, corresponding so exactly to Freud's diagram of the id, the ego and the superego, that it struck me of course as being rather pat and too easily accessible. We later discovered that the structure of his personality, as represented in the dream, and quite near consciousness, was rigidly maintained to protect him from much more primitive anxieties and objects. This may be why it was so easily represented and presented to me. Rosenfeld (1962) describes how an idealized, oppressive, and over-rigid superego can be internalized at the beginning of latency as a defence against underlying paranoia and depressive anxieties.

One can look at unconscious phantasy and the structures evolving out of it as determining the basic structure and character of the personality, as the matrix of our mental structure and life.

Klein's view of the early object relationships and primitive phantasies affected her views on narcissism. Freud himself wavered in his view about the earliness of object relationships. While his main line of thought, till 1920, postulates early phases of auto-erotism and primary narcissism, in other places he describes auto-erotism as a turning away from the mother's breast towards one's own body. He also states in his paper 'On narcissism' (1914b) that he has to admit that he never found any *clinical* evidence of the existence of primary narcissism.

Freud sees instincts as 'merely soldered to objects' (1905a, 1911). In Klein's view instincts are object-seeking and phantasies are about the relation between the self and the object. Even if on the surface a phantasy is apparently wholly narcissistic, on analysis it always manifests itself as containing an unconscious object relationship (Rosenfeld 1964a). For instance, the phantasy may be of oneself having incorporated, and become identified with, an ideal breast, or some later version of an ideal object, and this is accompanied by a projective phantasy of the distressed, angry or envious infant self being in others. Another common phantasy is of being inside, and having taken possession of, such an ideal object. This is illustrated by a very narcissistic patient who would either go into a dreamy, withdrawn state or act out in a manic way.[3] He would spend hours exercising in order to pile up muscles on his chest and shoulders. His dreams and associations would reveal that those muscles represented to him breasts. He had conscious sexual phantasies of getting into women's bottoms. They occurred frequently while he was exercising. There were more unconscious phantasies of getting inside his own bottom, felt as even preferable to women's bottoms. These states were invariably accompanied by feelings of persecution. He was forever fighting with intruders at work and at home. His dreams revealed the underlying unconscious phantasies. He often dreamed of *fortresses that were under siege.* In one dream, *a desert island he lived on was surrounded by cannibals in boats who were going to land.* He was narcissistically inside of and identified with me as mother (island), his depressed, intrusive, cannibalistic child self was projected outside. His awareness of his own destructiveness was minimal, and persecution was mainly dealt with by denial.

A typical dream: *He dreamed of a girl mime of his acquaintance. He saw her in the dream, miming a very gaudy figure. She was in a room with a funny ceiling, round, concave, and also gaudy.* The ceiling he associated both to a womb, because of its colour and gaudiness, and to the breast. He immediately recognized that the mime girl was himself since in the previous session he had spoken of his imitating me. So he phantasied he was both inside a womb/breast and being it. His very way of associating was partly an acting-in. He was interpreting the dream to himself, imitating me, and at the same time complying with what he thought I would say, so that he would be 'in my good books'.

The personality grows, matures, and develops. Growth and evolution of an individual are due not only to physiological growth and the maturation of the perceptual apparatus – memory, and so on – but also to accumulated experience and learning from reality. Learning from reality in turn is connected with the evolution and changes in phantasy life. Phantasies evolve. There is a constant struggle between the infant's omnipotent phantasies and the encounter of realities, good and bad.

The little girl who in the session could express her phantasies of a biting, spitting, dirtying 'lady on the wall' did not during the break have phantasies of a visual kind; nor dreams, as far as we know. She suffered from stomach pains and night fears which she could not describe. When she came into the consulting-room the phantasy became visual, and it was mistaken for a perception, a misperception close to a hallucination. In the course of development phantasies evolve from part-object relationships to whole-object relationships; from the predominance of most primitive oral, urinary, and anal drives to more genital ones.

But the evolution is not in the content of phantasy only. There is a simultaneous evolution from a concrete primitive perception to a differentiation between phantasy and reality perceptions. This evolution depends crucially on a gradual overcoming of the most primitive omnipotence through reality-testing, leading to increasingly realistic perceptions of one's self in the world. There is a constant struggle between the infant's omnipotent phantasies and the encounter of realities, good and bad. In the earliest and most primitive forms of feeling and thought, which Klein describes as the paranoid-schizoid position, the infant resorts to projective identification, omnipotently to alter the reality. However, from the beginning there is some reality-testing, and the mental life of the growing individual will be crucially affected by his capacity to recognize and tolerate the discrepancy between his omnipotent phantasy and expectation, and the reality that he encounters. This in turn will be affected both by the nature of the external experience being tolerable enough and the capacity of the infant to tolerate such discrepancies as he encounters. An angry baby with a phantasy of a persecuting breast may, to begin with, turn away from the returning feeding object, misperceiving it as bad. Some infants will never accept the returning object and they develop feeding difficulties. Others may, after an initial refusal, recognize the reality of the returning good object and accept the feed. And the mother's own capacity to tolerate patiently the initial refusal may affect the outcome. Expecting an ideal breast, which would return one to the imagined bliss of intra-uterine existence, the infant has to tolerate the breast that falls short of such an ideal.

But, even though reality-testing has to start from the beginning of life, the real battleground for the development of a mature relation to reality lies in the move from the paranoid schizoid to the depressive position. The depressive position has been described by Klein (1935, 1940) as the state of mind appearing in the infant when he starts relating to mother as a 'whole object'. Previous to that, the infant is in the paranoid-schizoid position (Klein 1946, 1952). This is characterized by a wholly egocentric 'part-object' relation, in which the infant perceives the object only in terms of his experiences split into good and bad objects, attributed to a good or bad breast respectively. Splitting, idealization, projective identification, and fragmentation predominate. In projective identification the infant projects not only his impulses but also parts of himself into the object, thus confusing the internal and external worlds. With a gradual withdrawal of projective identifications, together with a change in content and intensity of projection, a truer perception is established of mother as a separate person with her own continuity and characteristics, good and bad, and of oneself as having contradictory impulses, loving and hating, towards that person. This allows for the differentiation between oneself and the object, awareness of guilt, and fear of loss. In the earlier state of mind one could hate and wish to annihilate the bad object, and love, idealize, and keep the good one. When mother as a whole is felt to be omnipotently destroyed in hatred the needed and loved one is destroyed as well. New impulses appear – the wish to restore and regain the lost object – reparation. The implication of this shift is enormous and still being worked out (Spillius *et al.* 1989).

I have been particularly concerned with the implication of that shift on reality-testing and symbolism. There is a reciprocal relation between reality-testing and the depressive position: some reality-testing is necessary to initiate the changes from the paranoid-schizoid to the depressive position. Through tolerating discrepancies between his ideal and persecutory expectations and the encounter with the real object, the infant can gradually integrate the good and the bad, and perceive a whole object alternately or simultaneously as good and bad, loved and hated. And this kind of reality-testing paves the way to the recognition of his mother as an actual person with human characteristics rather than a part-object wholly related to himself. Once this change begins to happen, the change of orientation brought about in the child's mind pushes him to ever-increasing recognition of reality. An important part of reparative impulses in relation to the object is the withdrawal of projective identifications and allowing the object a separate existence. If this is achieved, omnipotence is diminished and the acceptance of the differentiation between the self and the object leads to the differentiation between the phantasy, which is a product of the self, and the reality, which is outside. And the objects that are internalized in phantasy and become such internal structures as the superego, become increasingly realistic. The nature of the phantasy changes from ideal and persecutory part-object relationships to whole objects such as the parental couple, siblings, and family, and the internal conflict worked out in phantasy is concerned more with reparation of damage done to those entities. It is also in the depressive position only that gradually repression replaces the more primitive defences of split-ting, idealization, and projection. The infant becomes more separate and differentiated from his object and capable of feeling guilty about his impulses and phantasies. He therefore represses them. And it is when repression functions that repressed impulses and phantasies can give rise to sublimation.

To give but one example, Patient A, a schizoid woman whose very disturbed mother had committed suicide when A was adolescent, had the following dream. *She dreamed of two balconies, one bathed in sunshine; one black and in gloom.* Her association was to a party in the castle of a foreign analyst in a foreign country which she knew her analyst attended; and the black balcony she associated to a joke that Dr S used to throw his patients down the cliff from his balcony. That patient tried to adhere to a rigid idealization of her analyst, to defend against a very persecutory situation. In her life she was rigid, relatively unproductive, and quite paranoid. She experienced her whole family as destroyed, fragmented, and persecutory. Many years after that dream, she had one in which *she was doing a jigsaw puzzle, and when it was finished it represented a house in a garden and a complete family on the lawn. It was very hard work but she was delighted.* Her associations were manifold. First, to her changed view of her family, having recaptured some memories of the time when it was happier and her mother was more accessible, to a jigsaw puzzle which she had accidentally knocked off, and to the mental activity of putting things together in the jigsaw puzzle. She said, 'It was like thinking – putting those together.' At the time of that dream she was writing a book, totally unconnected with her family or anything to do with it, but obviously her mental activity was felt to restore something in her mind felt as a home and a family. The change is not only in the content of her unconscious phantasy life; it is also a change in relation to her mental life, in that she now recognizes that her phantasies are a mental activity.

Higher mental activity, like thinking, is an interplay between phan-tasy and reality. We do not approach reality with a mind that is blank. We approach reality with expectations based on our preconscious or unconscious phantasies and experience reality, not only in infancy but throughout our lives, as a constant implementing and testing of our phantasies against reality. What is reality-testing? You can only test a hypothesis. Unconscious phantasies are like a series of hypotheses which can be tested by reality (Segal 1978).

In 'Negation', a paper in which Freud gives to phantasy a more fundamental role than in many other papers, he says:

The first and immediate aim therefore of reality-testing is not to find an object in real perception, which corresponds to the one presented, but to re-find such an object to convince oneself that it is still there.

(Freud 1925b: 237)

The richness, scope, and correctness of our mental activity is linked with our relation to unconscious phantasy. If unconscious phantasies are split off or too severely repressed, our conscious life is impoverished and restricted. On the other hand, if our reality-testing is impeded and the unconscious phantasies affect perception and dictate behaviour uncorrected by reality-testing, our mental life may appear to be rich but it is delusional (Segal 1978).

I think that the main thrust of Freud's thinking is that phantasy is not a primary activity. It has the same roots as, and is comparable to dreams, symptoms, parapraxes, and art; it does not underlie dreams, symptoms, thought, and art. For Klein, on the contrary, unconscious phantasy is a core primary activity, an original expression of both impulses and defences, and it is continually interacting with perception, modifying it but also modified by it. With maturation and increasing experience, the phantasies become more complex, with more differentiated sensory components and motives, and elaborated in various ways. Hence, for Klein unconscious phantasies underlie dreams, symptoms, perception, thought and creativity. They do not intrude into a dream; they are 'such stuff that dreams are made on'.

Unlike Freud's view that unconscious phantasy occasionally intrudes into dreaming, the view of phantasy that I present is that dreaming is but one of the expressions of unconscious phantasy. It has been noted by Freud that phantasies have the same unconscious content, and the same mechanism, the same formation, as dreams. One could say that they use the same language. When Freud discovered dream language and the dream-work, he discovered a dream world and a dream language which are with us whether asleep or awake – the world and the language of unconscious phantasy.

Notes

1 Patient described before in the *Introduction to the Work of Melanie Klein* (Segal 1964) at page 18.
2 Patient described before in the *Introduction to the Work of Melanie Klein* (Segal 1964) at page 20.
3 Patient described before in *Models of the Mind* (Rothstein 1985) at page 41.

3

Symbolism

It is not possible even to approach the topics of phantasy and dreams without the concept of unconscious symbolism. The discovery of symbolism and phantasy were interdependent and interrelated. Freud had discovered that hysterical symptoms had a meaning. They had a meaning in that they were a symbolic expression of underlying repressed phantasies. It is through symbolism that unconscious phantasy is expressed, whether in symptoms, in dreams, or in ordinary human relationships and endeavour. From the beginning, psycho-analytic work has been largely concerned with understanding the symbolic meaning of the patient's communication. At the beginning of his work, Freud used the concept of symbolism in this broad sense. He does so throughout his work on unconscious symbolism of hysterical and obsessional symptoms, and to begin with in his work on dreams; he speaks of symbol-formation (Freud 1900: 349-52). In the course of writing *The Interpretation of Dreams*, however, he introduces the term 'indirect representation', and begins to differentiate what he calls 'symbols' from other forms of indirect representation. In the second volume of *The Interpretation of Dreams* he says:

> When I had become familiar with the abundant use made of sym-bolism for representing material in dreams the question was bound to arise whether many of these symbols do not occur with a perm-anently fixed meaning. Like the 'grammalogues' in shorthand . . . I felt tempted to draw up a new dream book on the dictating principle.

And later:

> We must restrict ourselves here to remarking that representation by a symbol is among the indirect methods of representation, but that all kinds of indications warn us against lumping it in with other

forms of indirect representation without being able to form any clear conceptual picture of their distinguishing features.

(Freud 1900: 351)

He eventually comes to emphasize the following characteristics: that symbols are almost entirely universal; that they may vary in certain respects in different cultures; that they are given and not formed; and that they derive from an archaic past. In the dream he describes symbols as 'mute elements', in that patients have no associations to them and the interpretation has to be done uniquely by the analyst. Jones, in 1916, in his paper 'The theory of symbolism', based on Freud's work, starts by differentiating between conscious symbolism (which he unfortunately describes as metaphor) and unconscious symbolism:

1   A symbol represents what has been repressed from consciousness, and the whole process of symbolization is carried on unconsciously (Jones 1916: 97).
2   All symbols represent ideas of 'the self and of immediate blood relations and of the phenomena of birth, life and death' (Jones 1916: 102).
3   'A symbol has a constant meaning.' Many symbols can be used to represent the same repressed idea, but a given symbol has a constant meaning which is universal (Jones 1916: 97).
4   Symbolism arises as the result of intrapsychic conflict between the 'repressing tendencies and the repressed'. Further: 'Only what is repressed is symbolized; only what is repressed needs to be symbolized' (Jones 1916: 115–16).

He further distinguishes between sublimation and symbolization. 'Symbols', he says, 'arise when the affect investing the symbolized idea has not, as far as the symbol is concerned, proved capable of that modification in quality which is denoted by the term sublimation' (Jones 1916: 139).

Summarizing Jones's points, one might say that when a desire has to be given up because of conflict and repressed, it may express itself in a symbolical way, and the object of the desire which had to be given up can be replaced by a symbol.

This I think narrows the view of symbols even further, in that he considers that symbols are not part of sublimation. He is also more definite in the statement that the symbol has only one meaning, whilst Freud allows more flexibility (Freud 1900: 353): 'They frequently have more than one or even several meanings, and, as with Chinese script, correct interpretation can only be arrived at on each occasion from the context.'

Some of Jones's statements are very fundamental and up till today not controversial; namely, that symbolism at depth represents the 'immediate blood relations and the phenomena of birth, life and death'. His statement that symbolism arises as the result of intrapsychic conflict, that it represents what had been repressed, and that the whole process of symbolization is carried on unconsciously is also universally accepted. In other ways, however, later work has thrown doubt on some of his statements. For instance, does a symbol really have fixed meaning? For instance, one can see how many meanings may be packed into one symbol. Also, are there symbols that are given and do not necessitate psychic work and are therefore not part also of dream work? And are those symbols really any more mute than other forms of indirect representation? And, more importantly, do symbols really only appear in dreams or symptoms, and have no part in sublimated activities? Certainly, both Freud and Jones freely used the concept of unconscious symbolism in explaining works of art. And yet there is no doubt that there must be some fundamental difference between symbolism giving rise to symptoms or being expressed in a work of art. Freud had noticed that unconscious phantasy underlies both, but is it not also expressed in both in a symbolic way?

I think a new approach to the problem of symbolism came in Melanie Klein's work with children. She uses the concept of symbolism as it was originally used by Freud. She understands the child's play in the consulting-room as a symbolic expression of underlying unconscious conflicts, desires, and phantasies. Her 1923 paper, 'The role of the school in libidinal development', shows how she saw the symbolic expression of unconscious phantasy not only in the playroom, not only in the symptoms, but also in the child's everyday activities. For instance, she notices that to many children the school building symbolizes the mother's body and the teacher a father or a penis inside it. And in the consulting-room the child expresses his unconscious phantasy life in play that symbolizes it, and gives access to the analyst's understanding of the phantasy through its symbolic meaning.

She gradually developed a particular interest in the intellectual inhibitions of children, and attached great importance to the role of symbolism in intellectual development. In her paper 'A contribution to the theory of intellectual inhibitions' (1931), Klein equates intellectual inhibitions with an inhibition of the symbolic function, though she does not specifically spell it out. In her 1923 paper Klein still puts emphasis on libidinal trends and castration fears, strictly following Freud's ideas. As her work developed, however, she paid increasing attention to aggression and the resulting anxiety and guilt. She saw anxiety and guilt as one of the prime movers to symbol-formation. The child's epistemophilic instinct with libidinal and aggressive components gives rise to wishes and phantasies of exploring the mother's body. Anxiety and guilt due to the aggressive components lead to a displacement of the epistemophilic urge to other objects, thus endowing the world with symbolic meaning. But if the anxiety is excessive the whole process is inhibited.

In one of her most seminal papers, 'The importance of symbolformation in the development of the ego' (1930), she addresses herself specifically to an inhibition of symbol-formation and its catastrophic effect on the whole development of the ego. She described an autistic little boy of four, Dick, who could not talk or play; he showed no affection or anxiety and took no interest in his surroundings apart from door-handles, stations, and trains, which seemed to fascinate him. His analysis revealed that the child was terrified of his aggression towards his mother's body, and of her body which he felt had turned bad because of his attacks on it; because of the strength of his anxieties he had erected powerful defences against his phantasies about her. There resulted a paralysis of his phantasy life and of symbol formation. He had not endowed the world around him with any symbolic meaning and therefore took no interest in it. Melanie Klein came to the conclusion that if symbolization does not occur, the whole development of the ego is arrested. In this paper she concludes that excessive anxiety in relation to the mother's body and the onset of guilt bring about a paralysis of symbol-formation.

On re-reading that paper I was struck that what she describes in Dick's relation to his object is not only aggression but also a massive projective identification. She describes here a process which she conceptualized much later on. Dick in his phantasy attacks his mother's body by projecting into her what he feels to be his bad urine, faeces, and bad penis, representing also parts of himself. As a consequence, he sees her body as filled by bad and dangerous fragments of himself, and feels himself empty. The analysis of Dick must have been one of the important sources of her later formulation of the process of projective identification.

In my analysis of my first psychotic patient, Edward (Segal 1950), I was struck from the beginning by the nature of his concrete thinking – for instance, that words could be the same to him as objects. I had great difficulty in interpreting to him, because my words were experienced as things or as actions. For instance, interpreting to him a fear of being castrated would be experienced by him as my actually castrating him. In the same way, if he was angry with me in one session he would hallucinate my face as black with anger next day and shout for help to protect him from this 'black Indian'. I had at the same time a patient described in my paper (Segal 1952) 'A psychoanalytic contribution to aesthetics', who was a writer and frequently inhibited in writing when she started to experience words as broken-up bits of things. A border-line patient I had later on often could not read because she thought words were jumping out of the page and actually biting her eyes.

In 1957, in my paper 'Notes on symbol formation', I tried to tackle theoretically the problems of symbolic functioning I was struggling with in my clinical work. To help my understanding I used Klein's theoretical framework of the paranoid-schizoid and the depressive positions. At the beginning of that paper I described two patients, a hospital psychotic who since his illness had stopped playing the violin, and who, when asked why, answered with violence, 'Do you expect me to masturbate in public?'; whilst an analytical patient I had at the same time had dreams about playing the violin, also representing masturbation and associated phantasies which in no way interfered with his sublimation in playing the violin.

I came gradually to the conclusion that one could differentiate between two kinds of symbol-formation and symbolic function. In one, which I have called *symbolic equation,* and which underlies schizophrenic concrete thinking, the symbol is so equated with the object symbolized that the two are felt to be identical. A violin *is* a penis; playing the violin *is* masturbating and therefore not to be done in public. In the second case, that of true symbolism or *symbolic representation,* the symbol represents the object but is not entirely equated with it. To the patient who dreamed of the violin, the violin represented the penis, but was also differentiated from it, so that it could both embody unconscious masturbation phantasies and yet be sufficiently differentiated to be used as a violin as well, to make music which could represent intercourse but not be equated to intercourse. The move from symbolic equation to symbolic representation is beautifully described by Claudine Geissman (1990). She describes the evolution of the use the child made of little stones or marbles in the course of six years' analysis. This psychotic little girl started her analysis in the setting of a day hospital when she was eight. She could speak only a few words and could apparently understand the speech of others only a little. She could not play, and her main activities were to tear, break, cut objects, and kick and hit other children or adults. Any object she was interested in she would immediately put into her mouth or throw out. Often she put in her mouth little round stones, smooth and brown, and if she could get hold of them, small brown marbles. She also used them as missiles for hitting objects, human or inanimate. If she lost or mislaid one she would get into states of uncontrollable violence towards others and herself – tearing her hair and scratching her forehead.

She started her analytic treatment eagerly, and it appeared in her analysis that what interested her, and what made her follow the analyst to the treatment room, was the fact that the dress the analyst wore had some circles forming part of a geometric pattern in the fabric. Geissman traces the fate of the stones and marbles in the child's analysis. To begin with, the child used them in the way described, sucking them or spitting them out. In the course of the first few months she discovered in the lavatory that the lavatory chain was made of a succession of little metal balls. And she started to play with it. The main game was trying to put the lavatory chain as far as possible into her own throat and then to pull it out. Sometimes she would stroke the balls with her fingers. Dr Geissman thought it was an important move in the transference in that she related to something provided by the setting. The analyst understood the child's various activities in the toilet, as well as the game with the chain, as meaning that the child was treating the toilet and the chain concretely as the mother's body. She was trying to swallow the balls of the chain as a concrete equivalent of parts of the analyst/mother's body.

The first attempt which the child made at a symbolic representation was also connected with the marbles. She asked the analyst to draw for her a large grey marble. This was also her first complicated sentence, in that she could put together two qualities, *large* and *grey*. She crossed out the drawing with great satisfaction, but it was followed by a violent motor discharge, agitating her whole body.

In the next few sessions she continued to ask the analyst to draw the marbles, but she herself coloured them and kept comparing them with the marbles she would take out of her mouth. Gradually she started to draw them herself. She also asked the analyst to draw a variety of objects and to name them. Her vocabulary increased considerably during this time.

This seemed a first step in her greater ability to represent things symbolically. However, her symbols quickly became concretized, in that she would then proceed to wet the drawings and stuff them into her mouth. This process was linked with a variety of hypochondriacal complaints: fear of vomiting, of expelling poisonous gases, and so on.

But the phantasies that she expressed in the stones and marbles and in the drawing of them became gradually clearer, showing, for instance, a clear split between blue marbles (the analyst has blue eyes), which represented her love and an ideal breast; and the red and the black marbles, into which she projected violence, hatred, or despair. The drawings were still so concretely felt as part of herself and containing her feelings and thoughts that it was impossible for her to leave the room without taking them with her, which the analyst allowed since it seemed that if she left the room without them she appeared to feel completely empty of any thought, feeling, or capacity for movement.

Gradually she was able to shift her interest to other, similar objects – for instance, the necklace of pearls which the analyst wore, and eventually little rubber balloons that she blew up and then tore. At the end of one session she collected the debris of these balloons and asked the analyst to draw a whole balloon with the debris inside. This the analyst thought was the first time she tried to bring a whole, undamaged object together with the one that was broken or bad. And by making the good one contain the debris of the other she was making a step towards integration and reparation.

In the months that followed, the patient brought jacks, and added to them her little stones and marbles. And she started playing games with the analyst, using these objects as proper toys. This development in her way of using the little marbles was paralleled in the rest of her development. Now in the sixth year of her analysis, the girl can speak, read, write, relate to the other children, and play.

These very concrete methods of symbolization appear not only in the schizophrenic. They often underlie inhibitions, as in my writer patient.

Anthropological examples are sometimes very explicit. James Mooney, in 'The ghost-dance religion and the Sioux outbreak of 1890' (Annual Report of the Bureau of American Ethnology, XIV (2) (Washington, 1896); 721, 724), reports:

> An Indian prophet, Smohalla, chief of the Wanapum tribe, refused to till the ground. He held that it was a sin to mutilate and tear up the earth, mother of all. He said: 'You ask me to plow the ground! Shall I take a knife and tear my mother's bosom? Then when I die she will not take me to her bosom to rest. You ask me to dig for stone? Shall I dig under her skin for her bones? Then when I die, I cannot enter her body to be born again. You ask me to cut grass and make hay and sell it, and be rich like white men! But how dare I cut off my mother's hair?'

The Indian chief expresses here poetically what was the unconscious dilemma in my writer patient as well as the dilemma of many pastoral people forced into agriculture.

Concrete symbolization is conspicuously at the root of pathological mourning. If the dead person is felt as a concrete dead body, or as faeces, inside oneself, then normal mourning is not possible. It is only if the dead person can be felt as symbolically introjected and the internal object is symbolic of the lost person, that internal reparation, necessary to overcome mourning, can be achieved. An actually dead person cannot be brought back to life; nor can faeces be changed back into milk. It is only if the dead person is symbolically represented in the mind that the symbolic internal reparation can be done. Patient A, whom I quoted in the previous chapter, and who dreamed of putting together a jigsaw puzzle, said in her associations that it was a mental activity. Previously, among other difficulties, she had suffered from hypochondriacal and psychosomatic difficulties connected with a concrete phantasy of a fragmented dead mother and family attacking her body. It is only when the nature of her symbolism changed, as expressed in her dream of the jigsaw puzzle, that reparative internal work could be done, leading to a restoration of an internal family and the possibility of acceptance of the death of her mother and mourning. In her case the mourning had to involve the recognition of the real illness and associated badness of her mother, so different from the mother she wished to have, and only very seldom experienced. (Often such a recognition is even more painful than an actual loss.)

I have come to the conclusion that the two modes of symbolism pertain respectively to the paranoid-schizoid and the depressive position. Klein links symbolism with projection and identification. She says that she agrees with Ferenczi that symbolism starts with projection of parts of the infant's own body into the object. And yet her work on symbolism is mainly centred on introjection and reprojection. The child introjects and symbolizes the mother's body, and it is this internal mother that is then displaced on to the external world. Klein at that time had not yet worked out the actual interplay of projection and introjection. I think that in her later work her concept of projective identification threw a new light on the whole problem of symbolism. It struck me in my work that concrete symbolism prevailed when projective identification was in ascendance. This also seems logical. Symbolism is a tripartite relationship: the symbol, the object it symbolizes, and the person for whom the symbol is the symbol of the object. In the absence of a person there can be no symbol. That tripartite relationship does not hold when projective identification is in ascendance. The relevant part of the ego is identified with the object: there is not sufficient differentiation between the ego and the object itself, boundaries are lost, part of the ego is confused with the object, and the symbol which is a creation of the ego is confused with what is symbolized. It is only with the advent of the depressive position, the experience of separateness, separation and loss, that symbolic representation comes into play.

I would like to illustrate it with two extracts of material from a patient at about a two-year interval.

A neurotic young man, Patient C, is able much of the time to function on a depressive level. He can communicate in a symbolic way and has numerous sublimations. These achievements are, however, insecure, and at moments of stress he tends to use massive projective identification accompanied by a regression to concrete levels of functioning. Sometimes, for instance, he has near hallucinatory states of mind. He came to one session very perturbed because on waking up he had a hallucinatory experience. It differed from hallucination only in so far as he clung desperately to the belief that it must be the product of his own mind. When he woke up he felt his head was solid and he saw a motor-cycle riding into his head. The rider had a kind of mask on, which made his head look like a gorilla. He felt terrified and thought his head would explode. Then he looked at his own index finger, and got frightened because his finger looked like a gorilla. He only emerged from a state of acute anxiety when he made himself remember the previous session in which he was disturbed by a very intrusive noise of motor-cycles outside the consulting-room windows. He thought the motor cycles were connected with my son. He associated the gorilla to a psychotic boy who was described in a paper as looking like a gorilla. The finger was associated to anal masturbation, which he had spoken of a few days previously. His anal masturbation was always associated with violent projective identification into the anus of the analyst/mother, as described by Meltzer (1966). We understood that the motor-cycles outside the window represented his own intrusive self, identified with his finger and penis, projected into an external object, the motor-cycle of my son identified with it, and intruding into him. The same patient about two years later showed clearly in a dream how he felt this process of concretization had occurred.

One day he told me that, as he was going past my consulting-room door to the waiting-room, he became very anxious because the thought occurred to him that there was no guard at the door and nothing to stop him from getting into the consulting-room and interfering with the session of my other patient. Then he added, 'Come to think of it, there is nothing to stop me doing what I want on the couch. For instance, if I wanted to, I could lie upside down.' Then he giggled, and became embarrassed as he realized that upside down in the bed is the position he was in during some love play with his girlfriend the night before. So, apparently the situation was as follows: There is no guard at the door, no husband. He could have intercourse with me as his girlfriend and have our positions upside down; that is, with him dominating me – apparently, a plain Oedipal situation. He went on to tell me a dream. He said: 'I had a dream *in which I was explaining to M (the girlfriend) about my hallucinations. I was telling her, "Look, I dream up a car and there it is." And the car appeared.' He got into the front seat. But there was no partition between front and back — no pole to lean against. He started falling backwards, feeling an utmost panic.* And he woke up with severe anxiety.

My understanding of his associations preceding the telling of the dream, and the dream, was as follows. The pole is a phallic symbol. But also, I am of Polish origin, and he knew that my husband's name is Paul. In the absence of the pole, the father, or the penis in the vagina, there is nothing to stop him not just from having intercourse with his mother on a genital level, there is nothing to stop him from unrestrained projective identification with her, leading to the loss of boundaries, confusion, and panic. In this dream the father's penis is absent, but in other dreams or hallucinations, the persecutory penis would return, as in the hallucinations of the motor-cyclist.

What he seems to explain to his girlfriend in the dream is that when he projects himself into his mother, what used to be his thoughts, 'what he dreamed up', is felt by him as a reality in the external world. But the whole process, instead of hallucination at that point gave rise to a dream. It was subjected to dream-work which converted it into a meaningful internal and external communication. The dream-work has somewhat failed, since the patient woke up in a panic. Nevertheless, since the time of that dream his hallucination disappeared completely. I do not mean, of course, that that dream cured him like a magic wand. It represented the integration and assimilation of the insights acquired in our analytic work.

The aim of primitive projective identification is to deny a psychic internal reality by getting rid of a part of oneself and simultaneously possessing and controlling the object. A gradual change happens with the formation and use of symbols in the depressive position. Projective identifications are gradually withdrawn and the separateness of the subject from the object becomes more firmly maintained. With that comes a greater awareness of one's own psychic reality and the difference between internal and external. In such a situation the function of symbolism gradually acquires another meaning. Symbols are needed to overcome the loss of the object which has been experienced and accepted and to protect the object from one's aggressiveness. A symbol is like a precipitate of the mourning for the object. The relation between the capacity to symbolize and that of mourning is shown clearly by the same patient another couple of years after his hallucinations ceased.

After considerable change and improvement, the patient was getting married. Before his wedding, for which he was missing a few days of his analysis, he showed considerable ambivalence to myself representing the father. When he came back from his honeymoon he said that he had never been so moved in his life as he was at the actual wedding ceremony. He decided to marry in church in deference to his dead father, though he himself was not religious. He asked for his father's favourite hymn – 'The Lord is my shepherd' – to be sung at the wedding ceremony. He said that he had never in his life been so happy and so unhappy at one and the same time. He did not know if at that moment he was regaining his father or losing him. He was so aware of his father's presence in his thoughts, and so acutely aware of his real absence from the wedding. He then told me a dream he had had the night before in which *a fisherman was to take him out to teach him to fish. The fisherman's hands were bandaged because they had cuts on them. The patient was afraid that he would be too hurt to go fishing. But the fisherman assured him that he could still keep his promise.*

In the last session before the break I had occasion to point out to him that he was very cutting to me. I was the fisherman/father with the bandaged hand. The symbol is formed by the subject in the process of working through mourning. It represents the object but it is a creation of the subject and therefore it can be freely used. This is unlike a concrete symbolic equation, which is never felt sufficiently separate from the object for the subject to be able to use it freely. Also, in that the symbol is not equated with the object, the proper characteristics and functions of a substitute used symbolically are fully recognized and acknowledged. So that my neurotic patient, unlike the psychotic one, could recognize the violin for what it was, however much he needed it also as a symbol for an unachievable relationship.

Artists in particular, when successful, combine an enormous capacity for symbolic use of the material to express their unconscious phantasies with a most acute sense of the real characteristics of the material they use. Failing that second capacity they could not have used it effectively to convey the symbolic meaning they wish to embody.

I have summarized the differences between the two modes of functioning as follows (Segal 1957: 57):

I should like at this point to summarize what I mean by the terms 'symbolic equation' and 'symbol' respectively, and the conditions under which they arise. In the symbolic equation, the symbol-substitute is felt to *be* the original object. The substitute's own properties are not recognized or admitted. The symbolic equation is used to deny the absence of the ideal object, or to control a persecuting one. It belongs to the earliest stages of development. The symbol proper, available for sublimation and furthering the develop-

41

ment of the ego, is felt to *represent* the object; its own characteristics are recognized, respected, and used. It arises when depressive feelings predominate over paranoid-schizoid ones, when separation from the object, ambivalence, guilt, and loss can be experienced and tolerated. The symbol is used not to deny but to overcome loss. When the mechanism of projective identification is used as a defence against depressive anxieties, symbols already formed and functioning as symbols may revert to symbolic equations.

Symbol formation governs the capacity to communicate, since all communication is made by means of symbols. When schizoid disturbances in object relations occur, the capacity to communicate is similarly disturbed: first because the differentiation between the subject and the object is blurred, secondly because the *means* of communication are lacking since symbols are felt in a concrete fashion and are therefore unavailable for purposes of communication. One of the ever-recurring difficulties in the analysis of psychotic patients is this difficulty of communication. Words, for instance, whether the analyst's or the patient's, are felt to be objects or actions, and cannot be easily used for purposes of communication.

Symbols are needed not only in communication with the external world, but also in internal communication. Indeed, it could be asked what is meant when we speak of people being well in touch with their unconscious. It is not that they have consciously primitive phantasies, like those which become evident in their analyses, but merely that they have some awareness of their own impulses and feelings. However, I think that we mean more than this; we mean that they have actual *communication* with their unconscious phantasies. And this, like any other form of communication, can only be done with the help of symbols. So that in people who are 'well in touch with themselves' there is a constant free symbol-formation, whereby they can be consciously aware and in control of *symbolic expressions* of the underlying primitive phantasies. The difficulty of dealing with schizophrenic and schizoid patients lies not only in that they cannot communicate with us, but also with themselves. Any part of their ego may be split off from any other part with no communication available between them.

The capacity to communicate with oneself by using symbols is, I think, the basis of verbal thinking – which is the capacity to communicate with oneself by means of words. Not all internal communication is verbal thinking, but all verbal thinking is an internal communication by means of symbols – words.

(Segal 1957: 58)

42

I have presented two types of symbol-formation in a very extreme way. There is a long transition between the one and the other mode, and I do not think I have ever seen a patient the whole of whose function would be on a concrete level or whose concrete symbols would ever be completely concrete; only predominantly so. Nor do I think the symbolism of the depressive position is ever free of concrete elements. Any art, in particular, does embody concrete symbolic elements that give a work of art its immediate 'punch'; it has a concrete impact on our experience provided it is included in an otherwise more evolved type of symbolism, without which it would be no more than a meaningless bombardment. One of the great achievements of the depressive position is the capacity of the individual to integrate and to contain more primitive aspects of his experience, including the primitive symbolic equations.

Verbalization is a particular and highly evolved form of symbolism and I should like to show in some child material supervised by me the appearance of a verbalization in connection with reaching depressive anxieties. The eight-year-old boy was subjected to many separations due to the divorce of his parents. For the first six months of his analysis he hardly spoke. It was reported by his mother that at home he tended to be withdrawn and taciturn. He could work at school and play but his play was solitary. He played freely in the consulting-room and responded to interpretations by a change of expression or play. Occasionally, he briefly answered a question but never spoke spontaneously or freely. After some sessions before the ones I shall report, he would mutter a hardly audible 'thank-you' at the end of the session. I shall report briefly two sessions and more fully a third session in the six months of his analysis in which he started communicating and associating very freely in the context of mobilized depressive feelings.

On the Wednesday preceding a holiday he attached an aeroplane to a string and whirled it over his head. The analyst* interpreted that with the approaching holiday he may have thought she would fly away on a plane and he wanted to keep her and control her movements. He responded by saying spontaneously that his grandparents were arriving that day on a plane and went on associating very freely to their visit, which excited him. It appeared he was very fond of them and felt cherished by them. He also admitted some jealousy of his father, who, in contrast to himself, had a proper couple of parents.

On the Thursday he was very despondent. He tried to place strings on two pieces of furniture, but they kept falling between the two. He tried very unsuccessfully to attach the strings to the furniture. The

* Mrs C. Duthy.

43

analyst interpreted his despondency about people coming and going and of himself falling between the two parents. She said he felt it unsafe to attach himself to anyone. Towards the end of the session he cut a string into five bits and then made a knot between the two last ones. She interpreted that the five pieces of string were five sessions and that he did want to make a link between today and tomorrow and was less afraid of feeling attached to her. Throughout this session he did not talk, but at the end he was less despondent and smiled at her.

I shall report Friday's session more fully. When he came to the consulting-room he quickly went to his box and took out some long pieces of string which he had been cutting off a ball of string over the last few days. He took out his trains and his cars. Up till then he had always kept his coat on in the session. So the analyst commented on the fact that he was not wearing his coat and that she noticed that his mother was not with him in the waiting-room. In response to her comment he said that his mother had to go off, and at once busied himself with the pieces of string, placing them on the floor and around the room, hooking them over the furniture and hanging bits here and there. She said that things appeared to be very precariously tied together. Nothing was properly knotted and everything was in danger of slipping. She pointed out to him that it showed something about his relationship with her – how he liked to make only a loose connection with what she said, to speak to her would be to strengthen the tie with her which might make things difficult when they parted at the end of the session. At this he paused in his play and, turning to her, said: 'Our au-pair, Sophie, is going on the 10th.' She said, 'Oh, and how do you feel about that?' He replied: 'Well, it's OK because another one comes and replaces the old one – so I don't notice.' He paused a moment thoughtfully, and added: 'We've had lots – ten', and she agreed with him that it was indeed a lot for a boy of eight.

Now he set about playing again, making more loose connections with his pieces of string, though tying one piece a little more firmly across two low cupboards in the room. She said that it was best, in his view, to continue not to tie things down as it was simpler to make replacements, but she noted that the new piece of string appeared more firmly fixed and suggested that their talking together had put them on a firmer footing. As she spoke he was throwing some pieces of string over the line that he had just strung out, with a competent and business-like gesture. She said that he was now showing her how Sophie had looked after him, washing his clothes for him and hanging them up on the line. As he continued with his washing-line, flinging up the clothes to dry, she said that he would like so much to replace her quickly so that he did not have to feel sad at her going. He appeared quite oblivious of what she was saying, but then lost his balance slightly and bumped his head on the wall, adjusting himself quickly so that she would not notice his loss of composure and the pain of the bump. She showed him how the thought of losing Sophie was confusing and painful. He said Sophie looked after him very well.

He then began to play around with the trucks, putting them in a little pile and placing all the strings in a heap on top of them. He then lifted the trucks from under the strings and put them on the top of a shelf. Having done this, he swept all the trucks off the shelf and on to the floor. She said that she thought he was showing her that he was fishing with a net, that having caught the fish he was throwing them back into the water. He was very pleased and excited at her having understood, and immediately began to tell her how, on holiday in Italy, he had been fishing with his father. When they had caught the fish he had had to throw them back into the water. He explained that it would have been too expensive to keep them because they had to pay for the fish they caught and retained. Curious to see if the fish were alive when they were pushed back in, she asked if the fish swam away. He replied, 'Oh, no, they were half dead.' She interpreted his feeling 'half dead' when he thought she was throwing him away on her holiday. After a time he said that a few of them may be still alive and swam away if they were only half dead. She also interpreted that he felt it was too expensive and painful to think about Sophie and the analyst going away and that made him also throw away his feelings and the words that expressed them. But that he was also pleased that their talking together brought his feelings to life. At that he became a little anxious and she interpreted that he was immediately fearful of being sad at the loss of somebody.

There was a long quiet moment, and the child sat thoughtfully for a while. He began to play in a way that she had seen him do recently quite often, whizzing his cars over hillocks that he had made in the rug that he was sitting on. She ventured that he had been thinking about his holiday in Italy because that was where Sophie might come from, and he at once replied that she was Swiss but that Switzerland bordered on Italy. She then realized that he had been preoccupied with Sophie's leaving for quite some time, and she suggested that the whizzing over hillocks game represented skiing. First he objected, saying he had never been skiing and did not think about it, but afterwards, when the analyst suggested that he may have watched 'Skiing on Sunday' on TV, he said, yes, he very often watched it with Sophie, who loved skiing. He told her warmly that she was very nice and they talked a great deal about Switzerland together. The analyst interpreted that he was imagining that she would take him with her skiing.

45

As he spoke he began to gather up his cars and then his mood changed as he began to run them against the wall of the room violently. She said he was very angry with Sophie for leaving without him and with her too, as she would be leaving soon for the weekend without taking him with her. The weekend seemed to him like a cold, snowy place. He was particularly angry, as the fact that he had spoken to her tied a dangerous knot between them and it would not be so easy to feel that she was a new au-pair – like a new analyst on Monday. The patient stopped what he was doing abruptly and turned his back to the analyst. Suddenly she heard the alarm on his watch and she asked why he, such a punctilious boy, had set his alarm to go off three minutes before the end of the session, as it was then, and not at the end as usual. He replied that it had gone off by mistake, that he was setting it for ten minutes' time, the time he would reach home. She said that he was anxious about having been angry with Sophie and wanted to see her urgently to make sure that she was OK. She also pointed out that crossing from the consulting-room to his home was frightening, just as crossing from Friday to Monday left a dangerous gap.

What to me is striking and moving is how the little boy started associating freely and meaningfully when he was enabled to face his depression – anger and sadness at the partings. I think he was re-living the emergence of speech as part of working through the depressive position.

I think it is also significant that virtually his first free association (in the Wednesday session he spoke of the arrival of his grandparents who, unlike his real parents, are a properly married couple) on the Friday was to the fishing expedition with his father. I think it is significant that, though the actual material is about loss of the girl representing mother and the mother-analyst, it happens in the presence of the father and the analyst-father in the session. In the dream of my Patient C, who dreamed about falling into a car, the father's presence is needed to stop uncontrollable projective identification in relation to mother.

In the material of the little boy, the presence of the married couple and the supportive father-analyst seem to facilitate the problems of mourning in relation to his mother. It is an important aspect of the depressive position that the recognition of mother as a separate person includes the recognition of father as her partner, rather than as a part-object seen as her possession or as an object confused with her, as in the phantasy of the combined parents.

It has been recognized, particularly by Lacan, that father's penis to begin with, and then father, play a fundamental role at the beginning of language. His explanation, however, is very different from mine. I think one of the important functions of the father is that of an object seen as stopping a stream of mutual projective identifications between child and mother. When the depressive processes are initiated it enables the child to recognize the father as a separate object and that object in turn becomes a necessary factor in the further elaboration of the depressive position.

The changes in the nature of symbolism affect an evolution in one's experience of internal objects. I think Patient C's experience at his wedding shows this very beautifully. He is aware simultaneously of his loss of his father as a real external object and his regaining of a father as an internal object, but this internal object is not concrete as in pathological mourning; he is very aware that he regained him, as he said, in his thoughts. There is also an acknowledgement of his aggressive castrating wishes towards his father, but no projection of the aggression. The father remains helpful and supportive of his sexuality.

A similar awareness is shown by Patient A and her association to the jigsaw puzzle as being a mental process. When internal objects are felt in that way they can be projected into the external world, as in the case of my Patient C, into the helpful analyst as father, or, in the case of Patient A and her jigsaw puzzle, into writing a book that will bring together various elements symbolizing the bringing together of fragments of her mother and her family. It also allows for greater diversity because various aspects of the internal object can be symbolized by other events or figures in the external world without insistence on the object or situation being in all respects a substitute for the lost object.

Money-Kyrle (1965), in his paper 'Success and failure in mental maturation', emphasizes that with integration there is an increasing differentiation of the various aspects of the object, coupled with a capacity for generalization. Freud is reputed to have said that every man marries his mother, and yet some marriages are successful and fruitful; others are pathological because the wife is the mother. I think Freud was right that every man marries his mother, but the sanity or otherwise of such a procedure depends on the type and degree of symbolization. The wife may symbolize and contain some aspects of the mother; or she may be felt to *be* the mother, in which case the marriage carries all the prohibitions and conflicts of the relation to the mother.

In talking about phantasy and symbolism I want to emphasize the evolution not only of the content of phantasy but also of the level of symbolic function. Money-Kyrle, in 'Cognitive development', puts it succinctly thus:

To fit such observations the theory of conceptual development has to be extended to include not only growth in the number and scope

47

of concepts but also the growth of each single concept through at least three stages: a stage of concrete representation, which strictly speaking is not representation at all, since no distinction is made between the representation and the object or situation represented; a stage of ideographic representation, as in dreams; and a final stage of conscious and predominantly verbal thought.

(Money-Kyrle 1968: 422)

Once the step has been taken between concrete and depressive symbolism, the basis is also laid for further abstraction, including verbalization.

However, it does not follow that the capacity for purely abstract thought is of necessity a sign of mental health. It may be the result of splitting, in which abstract thought is completely devoid of emotional meaning. Indeed, with schizophrenics very often there is a simultaneity between crude concrete symbolization and complete abstractions, devoid of emotional, and sometimes even intellectual, meaning.

Once a higher mode of mental functioning has been achieved, it is of course not achieved once and for all. There is always a potential for regression. The more extensive the split-off area of unresolved psychotic conflicts, the more dramatic such a regression can be. In the typical schizophrenic breakdown in adolescence or early adulthood, the pressure of adolescent conflicts leads to a regression, to massive use of projective identification and an associated breakdown of the symbolic function. For instance, the capacity for speech, which has been acquired – and this I think implies necessarily that some depressive functioning has been achieved – gets disturbed and words themselves are treated as concrete objects.

A schizophrenic adolescent described by me (Segal 1957) when in a good phase of her illness wrote fairy-tales; in a bad phase, some of the fairy-tales 'came to life' and the figures she invented persecuted her. But in a less gross way those regressions occur momentarily in all of us. Patient C, even after his marriage and all it signifies, still frequently resorted to projective identifications of the kind described, though never to the degree of again being hallucinated.

What about symbolism in dreams? Money-Kyrle links dreams with the second stage of development, which he calls 'ideographs'. It is arguable that for the imagery of dreams to be formed at all a depressive level of functioning must have been achieved. Nevertheless, in some dreams, or some elements in some dreams, a regression occurs to concrete symbolization with all its consequences for the nature and function of the dream.

4

Mental space and elements of symbolism

In the previous chapter I presented my ideas on the development from concrete symbol-formation to the formation of symbols in the depressive position. My assumption was that concrete thinking and symbolization are a regression to the paranoid-schizoid position. Following Klein, I thought in terms of excessive projective identification as leading to pathology. Since then, more work has been done on the actual pathology of the paranoid-schizoid position, and the difference between more normal forms of projective identification, even before the depressive position, and forms which are pathological. In his paper on the 'Differentiation of the psychotic from the non-psychotic personalities', Bion (1957) distinguishes between normal and psychotic forms of projective identification. In normal development the projection is of parts of the personality or internal objects which are split off but not unduly fragmented; projections of that kind can be gradually withdrawn in the depressive position and re-owned by the self. The more pathological forms are characterized by a great hatred of reality and therefore also of the perceiving part of the ego, including its perceptual apparatus. The individual splinters this hateful part of the ego into minute fragments and projects it into the object with great violence, which in turn splits the object in a similar manner. The result is that the subject feels surrounded by 'bizarre objects'. Such objects are minute fragments of the subject's personality embodied in minute fragments of the object and imbued with extreme hostility. The existence of those bizarre objects in the mind can easily be detected in the psychotic, but they may also exist in a split-off part of the mind in non-psychotic people, particularly in the severe neurotic. In the case of more normal splitting and projective identification, projections are gradually withdrawn and integration is possible. Bizarre objects cannot easily be withdrawn, and the establishment of the depressive position is severely impeded. Also, unlike the ideal and the bad breast, and the good and bad parts of the self, which can be integrated, bizarre objects

49

cannot be integrated; they can only be agglomerated. (Such agglomerations are, I think, at the root of crowd phobia.)

Bion extended his considerations about the fate of projective identification to a theory about the formation of the mental apparatus based on the interplay between the 'contained and the container'. This interplay can take on a benign or a malignant character. At the dawn of life every infant tries to deal with his pains and needs by projecting them into an object. Projective identification is then in ascendance. What Freud describes as the 'motor discharge' in a normal infant I see as an expression of violent projective identifications.

I had a patient who dealt with being hungry by defecation, and had an elaborate theory to account for why he thought such a solution would work. But the persistent evacuation of need, pain, or hatred into the object, and then identification of the object with such projection, leads to the creation of a bad and fragmented object. This in turn leads either to a reintrojection of such an object, resulting in an increase of fragmentation of the self, or to attempts at blocking all introjection. We have always assumed that a good experience can modify the perception of the object and the self. The question is, what is the nature of this good experience? According to Bion, the good experience for the infant is that the containing object modifies in some way the part that had been projected into it. He describes how sojourn in the breast seems to ameliorate the projected parts.

> Melanie Klein has described an aspect of projective identification concerned with the modification of infantile fears; the infant projects a part of its psyche, namely its bad feelings into a good breast. Thence in due course they are removed and re-introjected. During their sojourn in the good breast they are felt to have been modified in such a way that the object that is re-introjected has become tolerable to the infant's psyche.
>
> (Bion 1952: 90)

This idea, that the projected part is modified by the action of the container, had been foreshadowed in Strachey's (1934) 'mutative interpretation'. Strachey says that the severity of the superego projected into the analyst is modified by the analyst's understanding so that its severity is diminished, and it can be re-introjected in a more benign form. However, Bion goes very much further in these considerations. According to him, at the first primitive stages of development, the infant is filled with raw perceptions, objects, and emotions. In *Elements of Psychoanalysis* he describes it thus:

> The infant suffers pangs of hunger and feels it's dying; racked by

guilt and anxiety and impelled by greed, it messes itself and cries. The mother picks it up, feeds it and comforts it and eventually the infant sleeps. Reforming the model to represent the feelings of the infant, we have the following version: the infant, filled with painful lumps of faeces, guilt, fears of impending death, chunks of greed, meanness and urine, evacuates these bad objects into the breast that is not there. As it does so, the good object turns the no-breast (mouth) into a breast, the faeces and urine into milk, the fears of impending death and anxiety into validity and confidence, the greed and meanness into feelings of love and generosity and the infant sucks its bad property, now translated into goodness, back again.

(Bion 1963: 31)

He calls those raw primitive elements 'beta elements'. Beta elements are raw, concretely felt experiences which can only be dealt with by expulsion. They are like a very primitive form of what I call 'concrete symbolic equation'. When those beta elements are projected into the breast they are modified by the mother's understanding and converted into what Bion calls 'alpha elements'. If the beta elements are felt to be concrete things that can only be ejected, the alpha elements on the contrary lend themselves to storage in memory, understanding, symbolization, and further development. They are the elements which can function in the symbolic way which characterizes the depressive position. If the interchange between the infant and the breast is good, then the infant not only reintrojects its own projections made the more bearable, but he also introjects the container-breast and its capacity to perform the alpha function; the mother's capacity to bear anxiety that is projected into her by the infant is crucial in this interplay. When the infant introjects the breast as a container that can perform what Bion calls the alpha function of converting the beta elements into alpha ones, it is a container which can bear anxiety sufficiently not to eject the beta elements as an immediate discharge of discomfort. An identification with a good container capable of performing the alpha function is the basis of a healthy mental apparatus.

This may seem to be very abstruse. Nevertheless, once alerted to it one can observe it in sessions, and its clinical relevance is enormous. I would like to show this in some fairly simple clinical material. I presented this material in another context[1] but I quote it here to illustrate the transformation of beta into alpha elements.

The mother of Patient D became pregnant when the patient was only four months old. Following the birth of the next sibling, the little girl turned her face to the wall and her back to her mother, and for quite a long period she did not relate to her mother at all. Later in childhood she had phases of mutism, though not of very long duration. The patient is not psychotic, but the existence of a split-off psychotic core in many ways interfered with her development.

A fortnight before the dream I shall report, she accidentally met me outside the consulting room in conversation with a young woman linked in her mind with her sister. During that fortnight she was persecuted; severely disturbed and her way of associating was completely different from her usual manner. The material she brought was fragmented, incoherent, sometimes nonsensical and it was thrown at me in a hostile, provocative, and disruptive way, making it almost impossible for me to think. Her communication was verbal as well as non-verbal, but the words were used as missiles, and the experience for the analyst was not of receiving a relevant communication but of being under real bombardment – the kind of behaviour described by Bion as a 'screen of beta elements'. I did, however, manage to make some contact with her, getting in touch with her distress and the violence provoked in her by the encounter and linking it with her preverbal experience of her mother's pregnancy.

After a fortnight she came one day in a quite different mood, and reported the following dream. *She dreamed about being in a session, and that she brought me a complaint. 'I mean I didn't talk about it, I actually brought it to the session. The complaint was I was shedding from inside my body all sorts of bits and pieces, little animals, maybe rabbits, bizarre fragments that could be more faecal. I thought (in the dream session) that the rabbits could be babies, but no, they were too bizarre. I was terribly anxious and I felt I was falling to pieces. You started explaining what was going on, but you conveyed that it could not be put into words. You painted for me a background and some figures. I wondered which was more important, the background or the figures. The figures became my parents. When that became clear I threw the bits at them and they – the bits – became dots. I wondered if it is an attack and I thought, yes, it probably is. Then you say: but the dots are also tears. I feel tremendously moved and not anxious any more and this is the first clear communication in words within the dream.'*

I shall not report her associations, though they were very relevant and enabled me to make a number of connections, because I want to concentrate on the 'container' and 'contained' aspect of the dream. I think the experience she showed me in the fortnight was of an infant who feels deprived of normal projective identification because she perceived her mother as already full with the next infant, and blocking it off. In fear and hatred she tries to project beta elements into me, standing for the pregnant mother, but she experienced me as blocking them; they rebound unmodified and she feels persecuted by what I say, feeling it as a return of hostile beta-element fragments. But gradually, as she finds that I neither collapse under the bombardment nor retaliate, nor block her out, she begins to feel that she is understood; and her experience alters, as she shows in the dream. The concrete complaints, bits falling out of her, become thoughts and feelings that could be put into words. But first the words must be supplied by me. Later on it also appeared that my painting in the dream was in a frame and the frame represented the psychoanalytic framework. The experience described in the dream is the benign interplay between the container and the contained, including a shift from beta to alpha elements, and it is conjoined with the move from the paranoid–schizoid to the depressive position.

The psychoanalytic setting, with its regularity of time and place, the supporting couch, and so on, is one of the factors in this containment. But the crucial factor is the analyst's understanding. It is when the patient feels understood that he feels that what he projected into the analyst's mind can be processed by that mind. He can then feel mentally contained. When, for external or internal reasons, this benign interchange does not happen its place is taken by a relation between the container and the contained which is mutually destructive or denuding.

I remember an experience right at the beginning of my psycho-analytic work which for some reason remained very vivid in my mind. A colleague working with an elderly psychotic woman asked me to see her on a Sunday to hold the fort between her sessions. She was obsessed with a childhood experience, and endlessly and repeatedly told me about it. A cruel gardener caught a horrible rat in a frightful trap full of teeth. She also hated her analyst, Dr R, and never wanted to see him again. I tried to talk to her about her feeling trapped in her analysis, and she said yes, Dr R was the cruel gardener with the trap. But when I said that she felt then like a rat in a trap she immediately countered that Dr R was the rat. Whichever way I tried to approach it I could not establish contact with her. Today I would have understood, theor-etically at least, that she was telling me that the only relation between the container and the contained can be mutual cruelty and destruction. I might have said that the only way she could visualize Dr R or myself and her coming together was in mutually attacking one another.

We frequently see patients, even non-psychotic patients, who experience any coming together as mutually destructive. I think the appearance of bizarre objects described by Bion belongs to this general category of relations between the container and the contained. In this case the container itself is split and, instead of the infant or patient experiencing that fragmented projections are contained by a container capable of standing them and the anxiety they produce, and bringing them together, the split bits of the container become part of persecution. The claustrophobic and agoraphobic anxiety frequently present in borderline patients can often be related to a bad relation between the container and the contained. The patient longs to be inside a room or a place representing mother, but that container is felt to have the projected characteristics of greed, envy or cruelty, and the claustrophobic anxiety forces the patient out, only to be confronted by agoraphobic anxiety of falling into a void – uncontained and disintegrating.

Bad relations between the container and the contained may be due to deficiencies in the maternal response, or they may lie more in the child himself. The failure in the mother may lie in her incapacity to tolerate the infant's projections. She may respond with hostility, by falling to pieces herself, or by blocking any projections. Sometimes the experience of a mother blocking projections or falling into pieces is part of the same pattern.

My Patient E was hard and brittle. At times she seemed so defended and hard on others that nothing could reach her; at other times she would collapse and feel that she was disintegrating under apparently minor provocations. She also suffered from great mental blocks. She often thought of herself as mentally deficient. She came to a session very distressed because at work she had been mildly rebuked for her inattention. Her boss had told her she was so preoccupied that at times it seemed as though she had no room in her mind for anything to do with her work. She then added, in a very distressed way, that she was the same with her children. While she was looking after her toddler he climbed on a ladder and fell, and it was as though she was not there, as though, 'in the words of my boss', she said, she had 'no room for him in her mind'. She also cannot spend much time playing with them or she feels they crowd her in. We have often seen with her how persecuted she feels by any demand when she is withdrawn. In the next session she was complaining bitterly about the lack of parking near my consulting-room. She was also very preoccupied with my recently having lost weight. She thought I had a heart condition. It appeared later that she was frightened of telling me anything painful or shocking because I might have a heart attack. This contrasted with her usual view that I was completely invulnerable. She told me she valued this view of me as invulnerable, and it was the only thing that made her analysis possible, since she did not feel me to be as fragile as her mother was. But she reluctantly agreed with my comment that this total invulnerability meant to her that talking to me was like beating her head against a wall, as though there was no parking room in my mind for taking in and feeling anything about her concerns. She had to maintain the idea of my invulnerability, however, because the alternative was that if she reached my heart I would collapse, and it might kill me. It seemed to me that much of what she was talking about in previous sessions – her own alterations between states of extreme hardness and total persecuted collapse and disintegration, was an identification with a mother experienced as narcissistic, unable to stand demands, criticisms, or aggression, and at the same time extremely vulnerable. It was guilt in particular, my patient thought, that her mother could not stand, and failure as an analyst with her is what she thinks I cannot stand, and yet this is what she relentlessly inflicts on me. Should I not be invulnerable, I would undoubtedly collapse and die.

In the next session she came very early and rang the bell wrongly (patients are supposed to ring my bell twice). When she came into the consulting-room she felt anxious about being so intrusive, being the first patient in the morning, and having rung the bell incorrectly, but not nearly as anxious as she used to be in the past. And she said, with great satisfaction, that coming early she found plenty of room to park. It seemed to me that the analysis of the previous days had given her some feeling that I could give parking space to her intrusions without either rejecting her or collapsing. (She could in fact be extremely intrusive.) E, in her material, shows her own experience as a child, but she also identifies with her mother and shows the state of mind of a mother incapable of tolerating the infant's projections.

In any situation when the child's projections are not well responded to, the child feels the return of his projections as made worse rather than better. In most cases both external and internal factors contribute to faulty development. On the part of the child, the interference comes from excessive envy. The child cannot tolerate his dependence on the maternal containment, and destroys it in his mind, with results at first sight not very different from those of an actual maternal failure. On many occasions, when E felt that I could tolerate and understand the various states of mind she could provoke in me, and interpret that to her in a way that made her feel contained, there was an initial great relief and improvement, promptly followed by envious attacks, at times quite annihilating the work done.

The clinical and theoretical implications of the understanding of this phenomenon are very wide, but I want to concentrate on that aspect of the concept of the relation between the container and the contained and the beta and alpha elements and the alpha function which are directly relevant to my theme of phantasy, symbolism, and dreams. The beta elements as described by Bion seem very close to what I called concrete symbolic equations. One could think that those equations are formed by beta elements. On the other hand, and I incline to that view, one could consider that the concrete equation is a transitional stage between the beta and the alpha elements. I think that, however concrete they are, they have certain qualities lacking in beta elements. For instance, they are not always minutely fragmented and are therefore more recognizable; their significance is more easily detected, and they have some symbolic meaning. The alpha elements, according to Bion, are elements of dream thought, myth, and symbolism, and I think that the alpha function is closely related to the symbolic function. Bion describes beta elements as 'saturated' through; alpha elements, on the other hand are 'unsaturated'. They are open to various 'realizations', in Bion's terms, or reality-testing and therefore open to many and varied transformations (hence there may be many symbols for one object or quality and, conversely a symbol may have many meanings). They lend themselves also to generalization, abstraction, and differentiation, a theme developed by Money-Kyrle (1968), in his paper 'On cognitive development'.

I have related the move from concrete symbolization to symbol proper to the move between the paranoid-schizoid and depressive positions. Bion considers the question of whether the move from beta to alpha precedes the depressive position, or whether it is the result of the shift. On the one hand, one could assume that there must be an alpha-function type of mental apparatus to be able to bear the depressive position. On the other hand, one could argue that the alpha elements could not be formed outside the depressive position. Bion speaks of a benign interchange in normal projective identification. However, one must take into account that the *identification* part of projective identification would preclude the kind of benign interchange that he describes. If the container becomes completely identified with the projected part, it disappears. A complete identification between the container and the contained probably occurs because of envy and the inability to tolerate the dependence on the container, and complete identification precludes the experience of feeling contained. This was very frequent with Patient E. After a good experience with me she could for a time become a perfect tolerant mother, but all link with me would disappear, and soon the identification would collapse. It seems to me, and I think this is a view to which Bion inclines, that the move from beta to alpha and from paranoid schizoid to depressive are conjoined phenomena which are interdependent. Some depressive dependence must be acknowledged for the experience of being contained to be admitted at all, but the internalization of that experience in turn facilitates the toleration of depressive anxiety. Thus the formation of alpha elements, and eventually proper symbols, are part and parcel of evolution in the depressive position.

Bion approaches separately what he calls the formation of the mental apparatus, which he links with the container–contained relationship and that of the occurrence of thoughts which have to be dealt with by that apparatus. He relates thought, as I have related symbolism, to the capacity to recognize and experience absence. To begin with, the lack of the breast is felt as a bad breast inside (hence my patient's conviction that he could get rid of hunger by defecating). It is only when the infant can recognize the absence of the object that he can either symbolize or think. Bion (1970) described it succinctly: 'No breast – therefore a thought'. However, to be capable of having such an experience there must be a part of the mind that can contain the anxiety of missing an object, a 'no-breast'. The container–contained relationship must have given rise to the creation of this part of the mental apparatus, without which even the thought 'no-breast' could not be formed.

According to Bion, the container–contained relationship determines the mental apparatus. He does not seem to link it with the concept of mental space, even though the container is essentially a spatial concept. I find it useful to think of it also as a way in which the mental space is formed and our experience of our minds, as Wollheim (1969) has pointed out, is always spatially tinged.

Using the words 'mental space' sometimes leads to confusion with Winnicott's concept of 'potential space' (Winnicott 1971), sometimes referred to as 'transitional space'. They are very different. For Winnicott the relevant space is the space between mother and child, which, if not intruded upon by the mother, is the space in which transitional phenomena develop and which becomes the cultural space. Bion's container or space is the result of interaction of projective and introjective identifications, and it is not just a neutral space but an active container with the capacity to perform the alpha function. This space is not between mother and child; it is an internal mental space formed by the introjection of a breast capable of containing the infant's projective identifications and giving them meaning.

Bion's concept of the container and the contained is strictly a two-body relationship, relating to the earliest relationship between the infant and the breast. However, if we think of the beginnings of 'no breast therefore a thought' or of the beginnings of symbolic thinking, and the shift between beta and alpha being a conjoint phenomenon with the depressive position, we have to ask ourselves about the status of the third object. It is implicit in the depressive position that the perception of a mother as a whole person implies the beginning of a recognition of her having a whole, separate life unrelated to the infant, primarily a relationship to the father. In fact, in his later work, Bion does refer to the place of the third object in relation to the relationship to the container and the contained.

In 'Attention and interpretation', Bion (1970) says that when there is a good relationship between container and contained it gives rise to a third object in a way that two objects share a third to the advantage of all three. In contrast, a bad relationship between container and contained gives rise to a third which is destructive to all three. I think that in the creation of such a bad object splitting also plays a part. In order to preserve the good relationship with the primary object, the breast, the infant splits off the bad relationship and projects it on to a third. I have described (Segal 1964: 57) a 'third area' due to this kind of splitting. In the chapter on the psychopathology of the paranoid-schizoid position, I speak of a borderline patient who said, 'Here is my head on the pillow, and there you are in your armchair, but between the top of my head and you there is nothing but horrible bloody mish-mash.' The other patient I describe in the chapter was a hebe-phrenic schizophrenic. In both those patients there was a third area split off from both patient and analyst containing bad fragments. The father, or more primitively the father's penis, easily becomes the ideal recipient of such projections.

My patient C, whom I described in Chapter 3 (pages 39–40), who suffered from transitory hallucinations, one day hallucinated a motor-cyclist driving in his head. He maintained a good relationship with me as mother by splitting off his hostile intrusive self and the bad part of me into a third object. He felt that as a child he could never be at peace alone with mother because of an intrusive elder sibling, and according to his mother his breastfeeding was also disturbed by his father's demands on her. The hallucination itself was due to a splitting process in which the bad, mutually intrusive relationship between himself and me was split off into a hallucination.

The appearance of a third object is the beginning of the realization of the existence of the father in the Oedipal triangle. R Britton made an interesting extension of Bion's concept of the container and the contained to include the relationship with the father:

The acknowledgement by the child of the parents' relationship with each other unites his psychic world, limiting it to one world shared with his two parents, in which different object relationships can exist. The closure of the Oedipal triangle by the recognition of the link joining the parents provides a limiting boundary for the internal world. It creates what I call 'triangular space', i.e., a space bounded by the three persons of the Oedipus situation and of their potential relationships.

(Britton 1989: 86)

Britton, like myself, sees the container as being also related to mental space. This new space has new characteristics. It contains three kinds of possible relationships, the vertices of the triangle: the relationship between the mother and the child; that between the father and the child and that between the parents from which the child is excluded. Each of these relationships can be seen as mutually beneficial, the third – excluded – not being necessarily a hostile entity, unlike the father and sibling of my Patient C, or another patient, who dreamed *that a man* (obviously related to his father) *comes into the kitchen to steal all the food.* This extension of the mental space is crucial for the perception of a variety of relationships, not mutually exclusive or necessarily hostile to one another. The third can become an objective and/or benevolent observer. This observing part is a necessary feature in mental life for the existence of insight, benevolent curiosity; it is the basis of a constructive, epistemophilic attitude.

Two dreams of a patient in an advanced stage of her analysis illustrate some features of this triangular space. The first dream follows an event in the transference. I asked the patient, K, if she could come ten minutes earlier for her session. She gave me apparently good reasons for not being able to change her time. As I had unavoidably to leave my consulting room at the earlier time I had to tell her that I was sorry, but I would have to cut her session ten minutes short. It soon transpired that in such a case she could think of ways of coming ten minutes early. The next day she had the following dream. *She was walking down a lovely road bordered by leafy trees. But she came to the end of the road. There was no way to go on. She retraced her steps, and on the way she saw a clearing, and in that clearing a couple were having very vigorous sexual intercourse. The intercourse was not only physical. The man seemed to have been telling the woman how passionately he loved her. She observed this scene with great interest.* Her first association was to tell me that there was nothing voyeuristic or exhibitionistic about the scene. The couple were making love in a clearing in a forest. They were concerned with one another, not exhibiting. She had no voyeuristic excitement. She did not seek to see them, unlike in some other dreams, and she was just interested, not excited. She associated the end of the road to my firmly telling her that I wished to end the session ten minutes early.

I think that the leafy road which she enjoyed so much represents her phantasy of being inside me controlling me, a very common psychic stance in her. The frustration about the end of the session shows her that this has come to an end. She sometimes uses the expression 'No way!'. 'No way' can she maintain the phantasy of being inside and controlling me. When she gives up that phantasy she is confronted by another space which opens a clearing in which the parental intercourse happens. And in the dream it is unspoilt by voyeuristic projections.

Further work of course led to the recognition of repressed feelings of jealousy and rage, and she had to make room in her mind for those feelings as well. But it is important that she could be also an objective and appreciative observer.

Some time later she had a similar dream, bringing another aspect of the new space and a new way of relating. In the dream *she was in the kitchen with me, washing up. We were talking about marriage, and I was telling her that I married a Pole because Poles are so passionate*. In that dream her relation to me in terms of feeding and washing up is not spoilt, and is even enriched, by her knowledge of me as part of the couple. Similarly, her relation to me as mother does not disturb her own appreciation of father.

A patient of mine, F, is tormented by recurring panics. Though intelligent, when in a state of panic, whether conscious or unconscious, she loses her concentration and all ability to think. In one of the sessions she described acute anxieties about a hole in a wall. Some building work had to be done in her house; she could not imagine it being done without a big hole in the wall. She thought her children could fall through the hole, or herself, and anyway the thought of this big black hole put her in a panic. It was fairly clear in the session that she had no idea in her mind that the builder might know what he is doing. (The transference implications were obvious.) When this was interpreted she told me that she had another panic which assailed her on the way to the session: she had lost her diary which had confidential information about herself and the work in her office, involving other people, and the loss of the diary could be catastrophic. It slowly emerged that the loss of the diary had to do with her having read a poster of a lecture I was giving, jointly with a man. She did not intend to attend this event, but she also wanted to forget the date, not to be troubled by it. The indiscretion referred to was what she felt was the indecency of my exhibiting myself on a platform with the man.

The next session was very difficult, and analytic work was hardly possible because of the patient's determination to break any links. Two themes seem to have emerged: one of an internal tormentor. It eventually led to a phantasy of a hand cruelly squeezing out a breast that was filled with a boil. The second theme referred to sexuality. She felt that I and others were trying to impose on her a view of sexual intercourse as something pleasurable and non-destructive, which was a denial, and idealization, since 'I thought everybody knew that sex was always sado-masochistic'. Another view she had of sex was as of two people coming together in intercourse in cruelty to the third person in front of whom they were exhibiting, so as to inflict on this third person unbearable feelings of exclusion, inferiority, and jealousy. Some links could be established – for instance, the parents-myself cruelly exhibiting to the child and the resulting destruction of her relationship to the breast; but the patient remained on the whole disconnected from me, angry, and very anxious.

In the third session, as she was speaking of the hole, some music from the neighbouring flat could just be heard in the consulting-room. She drew my attention to it, and said it made her think of people dancing. She did not feel disturbed or persecuted by it. Eventually we could establish that the terrible hole in her mind was the missing space in which she could perceive the parents, represented by me, dancing together. Later in the session, she started speaking about her difficulties in writing a report she had to do at work, but in a much quieter and understanding way. This patient had an idealizing relationship to the breast, but this relationship was very fragile, only to be maintained by a splitting off of ambivalence. The appearance of a third object turns everything into torment. Not only is she tormented by phantasies of sexuality infused with cruelty, but the original relation to the breast is destroyed by this intrusion and also turns into torment. When this intrusion happens her mind becomes itself disjointed and fragmented, and she becomes filled with intense paranoid and hypochondriacal phantasies. At those points her capacity for understanding and symbolization gets lost. My talking to others is experienced as my forcing her to witness an actual sexual intercourse. The bad feelings about me become a tormented and tormenting, poisonous breast inside her, experienced in her physical symptoms. She can get rid of the resulting persecution by making a hole in her mind instead of a space accommodating the dancing parents.

The fear experienced by the patient, F, of the hole in the wall is similar to the fear in the dream of Patient D described earlier, in which she brings me her complaints as bits and pieces falling out of her body, among them something that could be children. She brings her complaints as bits and pieces falling out of a hole in her body. What she represented at the beginning of her dream is very similar to Patient D's fear about the hole in the wall through which the children would fall out. Though later in the dream D shows how the containment and understanding provided by the analytic situation led to a transformation of beta into alpha elements. Patient F shows the change in the third session. Another patient, less severely disturbed, exemplified clearly the effect on thinking of a difficulty in establishing the triangle.

She started the session by telling me that she had two very tiny fragments of a dream. In one, *she saw me surrounded by middle-aged, stupid, altogether despicable men.* Of the second fragment she could remember only that it had something to do with African land and African people. The first dream seemed to both of us pretty obvious, with an impending long weekend. But the hardly remembered, fragment of the dream brought surprisingly rich associations. To begin with, she expressed again her horror of racial prejudices from which she cannot free herself, and which she detests in herself. That seemed to provide a link between the dream of men with whom I may spend my weekend and the one about the Africans. But her other associations were more unexpected and illuminating. The patient is a form teacher, and she started speaking about a child's difficulty in learning any grammar, particularly foreign grammar. She thought that Africa might represent what this girl feels about foreign grammar as totally exotic and incomprehensible. This child, she said, is quite clever, but very disjointed. She seems unable to make certain connections, and this seems particularly obvious in her total inability to grasp the rules of grammar. After all, grammar, with the sort of patterns it describes, should come more naturally. Then she laughed, and said, 'Maybe to her grammar is so foreign and exotic – just like parents in intercourse must appear to the child – beyond reach, incomprehensible, exotic, foreign.' This patient is often preoccupied and disturbed by very primitive fantasies of the primal scene. In this session she seems to feel that there are certain natural patterns of interrelationships, as in grammar (shades of Chomsky!), and that this includes an intuitive awareness of parental intercourse.

In the first dream that intercourse is attacked and derided. She has a prejudice against it, like a prejudice against Africans. And her associations to it suggest that she is aware how her thinking is dislocated by her attack on those natural patterns of relationships.

I think that the triangular space is also like the space for a new baby. It is not 'saturated' by the mutual projections between the mother and child. As a new, unsaturated, mental space it allows for the birth of new thoughts: two can come together like parents in intercourse to produce a third new thought.

The various considerations I have brought in about the relationship between the container and the contained, and extension of that concept to include the mental space which accommodates the parents together, and the potential new baby, seem to be far removed from my general theme of dreams, phantasy, and symbolism. I think, however, that they are crucial in the understanding of the mental processes involved in the formation of phantasy and dream thoughts and the malfunctions of the mental apparatus which account for its pathology.

Notes

1 Patient described in 'Early infantile development as reflected in the psychoanalytical process: steps in integration' (Segal 1982).

5

The dream and the ego

In previous chapters I put forward the idea that a dream is a way of expressing and elaborating an unconscious phantasy. What Freud called a 'compromise' takes the form of a wish-fulfilling phantasy, satisfying contradictory wishes and defences. That phantasy is expressed and further worked through in the dream. A dream performs many functions. It provides a phantasy expression of an unconscious conflict and seeks a phantasy solution – wish-fulfilment. Dream-work is part of the elaboration of unconscious conflict. It provides also an intrapsychic communication between the unconscious and the conscious. When we remember a dream we retain communication with symbolic expressions of the unconscious. In the analytical process this internal communication becomes also a means of communication with the analyst.

In Chapter 1 I commented on how great is the task of the ego in accomplishing psychic work – dream-work – involved in dreaming. And I raised the question of what happens to dreaming and dreams when the ego is temporarily or permanently not capable of carrying out the tasks involved in producing a neurotic or a normal dream. In the acute psychotic there is often no distinction between a hallucination, a dream, and a real event. I remember sessions early in the treatment of an acute schizophrenic, when he would give me a jumbled account of his night in which it was impossible to tell what really happened, what he hallucinated whilst awake, or what he hallucinated whilst asleep. Bion describes a patient who was terrified because he had dreamed of his analyst and therefore concluded that he must have devoured him, and was amazed to find his analyst alive in the real external world. In such cases, the patient is unable to differentiate between the psychic event which is a dream and actual events in the external world.

In the less acute cases in our daily practice, we find patients whose dreams occasionally or habitually do not fulfil the dream function as described by Freud. The dreams of these patients serve the function not of elaborating and symbolizing latent dream thoughts, but the function of getting rid of psychic content (Bion 1958). In the analysis they serve predominantly not for communication but for acting-in. That is, such dreams function not as symbolic communication but as symbolic equations, or beta elements which are expelled. Dreaming is thus felt as an expulsion and is sometimes equated with actual urination or defecation. In the session the patient projects into the analyst with various consequences. Though the aim of such projections is not usually intended as a communication, if the analyst can understand them they become a communication as well. Mr H[1] dreamed profusely. He had numerous notebooks in which he would write down his dreams and associations. He would report them to me sometimes on the following day, but often weeks or months later he would produce the notebook and start reading from it. Mr H was a past master at getting rid of his psychic life. For instance, after the session he would spend hours in the lavatory defecating and carrying out what he called his 'post-analysis', which was his way of getting rid of any feeling or insight he might have experienced in the session. His dreams served a similar function. Whatever touched him could give rise to a dream which would be defecated into his little notebook and in that way disposed of. In his case it was often the more insightful part of himself that was thus disposed of. This was particularly marked after the death of his mother, when he had several dreams expressing his mourning. The dreams were duly recorded and forgotten, reported to me weeks later, whilst in his conscious life he seemed untouched by mourning. In *An Outline of Psycho-analysis*, describing the splitting in the ego in psychosis, Freud (1940: 202) speaks of a psychotic patient in whom the split-off, more sane part of the ego was functioning whilst dreaming.

Borderline patients like Mr H differ from those psychotics who cannot differentiate at all between dream, hallucination, and reality; they know they have dreamed, they speak of their dreams, but in spite of that their dreams are psychically equivalent to concrete events, and they have similar consequences. Miss G[2] would start a session complaining that my room smelled of gas. We would find subsequently that she had dreamed of gas balloons exploding. If, in her dream, I or a character standing for me persecuted her, she would upbraid me for it, as though the character in the dream was actually myself. She had a similar waking phenomenon. She had numerous fantasies which she called 'fantasies', but she lived them as though they were hallucinations. For instance, she walked very awkwardly because she had a phantasy faecal penis stuck in her vagina or in her anus. What she called a fantasy was nearer to a psychosomatic hallucination.

When patients use dreaming for evacuating mental contents, the process can take many forms. Sometimes the dreaming itself is felt to accomplish the evacuation, or the recording of it, as in the case of Mr H's notebooks. Very often it is dreaming and telling the dream to the analyst that accomplishes the evacuation. The telling of the dream may be devised to rouse feelings in the analyst and thereby accomplish a projective identification. Mr H sometimes told me dreams of torture or terror which shook me, whilst he seemed to have no feelings about them whatsoever. Also, some of the dreams about his mother's death could evoke in me a feeling of being very moved, which contrasted with a total lack of feeling in himself. The evacuation is into an object, and in the analytic situation the object is the analyst. The aim is twofold: one, to split off and get rid of certain psychic contents; and two, to affect the object. For Mr H, the getting rid of content was usually the primary aim and the way it affected his object often secondary.

In Mr M, on the contrary, the aim of affecting the object was the more prominent. At the beginning of his analysis he used to flood me with dreams and numerous associations. When I pointed out to him his inability to listen to the interpretations and the way his numerous associations, with which he interspersed the telling of the dream, were in fact obscuring the meaning, rather than helping me to clarify the dream, he was very shocked and surprised. He said he thought that was how one analysed dreams – 'Isn't that how Freud analysed his Irma dream?' It soon became apparent that he was being Freud, analysing his own dreams with me as his dazzled and mesmerized audience. After some analysis of this meaning of his way of dreaming and recounting his dreams, he produced a few shorter dreams with more coherent and pertinent associations. Those dreams, and the associations to them, dealt with and illuminated the psychic function of his dreaming and recounting the dreams.

He dreamed that *he was injecting anti-rabies serum into a big football. It was important that not a drop should touch him. He was also carelessly putting something into a woman's purse.* He associated to his promiscuity and seduction of women – an activity which he wished to see as reparative (the serum) – but which was, in fact, destructive and projective. He had a conviction that when he approached a woman, he had the power to implant in her what he called 'the need for M', thus projecting his own infantile need into the woman. Once so infected, only intercourse with M (the serum) could save them. But the injection by his penis was re-infecting them – getting them more addicted to him. The serum in the dream is destructive and not a drop must touch him. This, of course, is also a reference to analysis. He injects his dreams into me, but not a drop of an interpretation must touch him.

The next day the situation became even clearer. He washed his hair just before the session and literally soaked my pillow. He had a dream of *piercing a balloon and making it burst*. 'It popped like a cherry.' He associated this dream with the previous one of injecting the football. It had become clear that for him his profuse dreams and his way of telling them to me were like a stream of sexualized urine, meant to dazzle, seduce, confuse me, and make my mind burst. He was motivated both by his need to get rid of his own infantile needs and by envious rivalry with me. He was Freud in the sessions. (Note also the theme of injection continuing the identification with the Irma dream.)

Sometime later he brought four dreams. I shall not give them in full, since the telling of dreams and the associations took nearly the whole session. The first dream referred to masturbation; the second to an injunction that one must not fuck one's daughter, the fourth one referred to Othello's killing of Desdemona. But it is the third dream which is relevant to my theme. He dreamed *that he was putting tiny fragments of something into two oval shapes which became warped. He was also trying to bring them together.* He interrupted himself to associate that the shape reminded him of a grapefruit, since later in the dream *he was buying a grapefruit from a woman and was annoyed that the price had been raised.* (His fee had been raised shortly before this.) He thought the small fragments were his disintegrated dreams and that he hoped that putting them in the oval shapes and bringing the shapes together meant he was integrating them. He used an expression typical of him – 'I want it to mean that' – then he continued the dream. *He was running in a transparent warped passage. There was a supervisor at the entrance who might not let him into the place he was running to. Then came the grapefruit part. Possibly he had to buy a grapefruit from a woman to get in.*

I think that in this dream it is the *warped* grapefruit and the *warped* corridor that are the essential clues. The other three dreams contained fragments of a fragmented and projected Oedipal situation – for instance, projecting his Oedipal feelings into his daughter. In the third dream he shows how putting his dreams into me – the oval shapes, the breasts, the grapefruit he has to buy – he is both projecting a fragmented Oedipal situation into me and warping my judgement. His 'I want it to mean' is also his wanting me to interpret the dream's meaning to be what he wants it to be, so that I would let him 'into the place'. Dreaming and telling me dreams were experienced by him as an actual urinary intercourse in which he both projected parts of himself into me and wished to affect my mind – burst it, as in the previous dreams – or warp it. His conviction that he could affect my mind that way led to his tendency to experience his analysis as a *folie à deux*, reproducing his experience with his mother, who erotized her relationship with him and idolized him in a virtually delusional way. Dreams were, of course, only one of the manifestations of this process, but a very central one.

I also think that the two oval shapes were also his own lungs, since the re-internalization of the destroyed breasts was, I think, at the root of the asthma from which he occasionally suffered.

When people experience dreams as concrete events or objects, a stool, anal gas, or a stream of urine, which are expelled into an object, their reality perceptions are unavoidably affected. I have described how Miss G would complain that my room smelled of gas, and only later we would find out that she had a dream in which a gas balloon exploded. When she had a quarrel in a dream, I was perceived as a quarrelsome person. The dream obviously spilled into her perception of reality. An example of such misperceptions was reported to me by a colleague*, in a patient I was supervising.

The patient started the session by saying that he was very worried because he thought his analyst had shaved his beard, but he could not be sure. Later in the session he said that in a certain light he could see his own face reflected in the lamp overhead. Other associations dealt with his intrusiveness into the analyst's mind and his fear of getting confused with the analyst. At that point the analyst drew his attention to the fact that if he could see his own reflection in the lamp he could also see the reflection of the analyst's face. The patient was amazed. He looked again and said he had never noticed it before. He only saw his own face. But he still could not see whether the analyst had shaved his beard. The patient's projective identification, seeing only his face where he should have seen both, prompted the analyst to ask whether the patient himself had thought of shaving his beard. 'No, he hadn't,' but he suddenly remembered that he *had dreamed* the previous night that he looked into the mirror and that his own beard was shaved. It seems that his dream was completely expelled into the analyst with the effect that he perceived the analyst's face the way his own face was in the dream.

This case shows a striking sensory misperception. My patients – Mr H, Mr M, Miss G – showed similar occasional misperceptions. But the distortion of the perception on the emotional level, like Mr M's experience of the *folie à deux*, is invariably present. In addition, all the dreams of the kind I have reported are also to a large extent acted out in the session: Mr M's rapid confusing and confused way of reporting dreams, his wetting the pillow, Miss G's quarrels with me, and so on.

In certain patients, however, or in some patients at some times, the

* Dr R. Britton.

acting-in is the most prominent feature. The dream has to be acted out in detail in the session. For instance, Mr H had numerous dreams in which he would be late for a meal or a meeting, a precise number of minutes – anything from two to forty-five – and then he would come late to the session by exactly the same number of minutes.

A patient whose analysis I supervised[†] showed a similar mechanism. In a recent session he took half an hour on procrastinating, empty associations. Then he produced a dream in which *he arrived at a zebra crossing at 8.20. There was a policeman and an incident. He did not want to see the incident and walked away.* The analyst glanced at her watch and it was precisely 8.20. Then the patient let his associations wander away from the dream. As in the dream, he wandered away from the incident he did not want to see. The session as such was a re-enactment of the dream.

Miss G had a number of dreams of paranoid quarrels with thinly veiled parental figures. When this happened she would start a kind of quarrel with me in the session. Whether I was silent or whatever I said would be interpreted by her as quarrelling. I felt like a puppet in someone else's nightmare. Eventually we would find that she had had a dream and was acting it in the session. In these cases I have a feeling that the dream content has to be evacuated by a very precise re-enactment.

I have called this kind of dream a 'predictive dream', because it seems to predict future happenings as they are almost automatically acted out. They function like a 'definitory hypothesis', described by Bion (1963). Such dreams are often also acted out outside the session. The more usual analytic experience is that when a patient brings a dream and we deal with it in the session he is less compelled to act out. It is not so with predictive dreams. These seem to be more like blueprints for future acting out, both inside and outside the session. This was particularly striking with Mr H. If he brought a dream indicating a wish for a homosexual acting out as a reaction to the weekend break, no analysis of the dream would prevent his carrying out the action almost precisely as planned in the dream. It could of course be the effect of the analysis being incorrect or insufficient. But I also had the impression that no analytic understanding could contain the powerful urge to get rid of the dream content by acting it out precisely. Of course all dreams are to a certain extent acted in and out. Or rather, the phantasy expressed in the dream is to a certain extent acted in and out in what Rosenfeld (1964b) described as 'normal acting out'. However, the dreams I am speaking about in this chapter are

† Analyst, Dr Piontelli.

predominantly used for acting in and out, and in the case of predictive dreams this is particularly compulsive and often uncontainable in the session.

Those dreams in which the dream-work has partially or completely failed are characterized by interrelated phenomena. One, which is not always present, is a certain crudity in symbolization. For instance, Miss G would regularly dream of houses where there was a restaurant on the first floor, a gas boiler or a furnace in the basement at the back, and scenes of sexual violence or murder in the basement at the front. Or she would dream of two wasps in sexual intercourse which consisted of urinating or defecating into one another, and so on. Mr H, who hunted guardsmen for sado-masochistic sex, would dream of a guardsman pursuing him with a red-hot poker. It is as though the barest minimum of effort went into symbolization. Other features are constant: the experience of the dream as a concrete event, the use of the dream for the expulsion of psychic content, and the associated blurring of boundaries between internal and external worlds. The burst balloon of Miss G is not felt as an inner mental event. It invades her perception of my room. It is equally clear in the case reported by Dr Britton: the dream is not even remembered, it becomes part of the analyst's face.

Freud speaks of the dream as a harmless psychosis and also as of a hallucination happening during sleep. I do not think that this applies to most dreams. I think that hallucination is a pathological process linked with pathological projective identification. The kind of dreams that I am describing here are indeed like hallucinations happening during sleep. But in the normal dream, where the process of repression, symbolization, and working-through is achieved by the dream-work, the dreams, even though they are pictorial representations of a phantasy, do not have the psychic function of a hallucination.

The benign interplay between projection and introjection, which occurs when there is a constructive relationship between container and contained, is at the very basis of the mental functioning, including dreaming. The failure of a good relation to an internal container leads to the concretization of mental events.[3] *No DREAM SCREEN*

An example comes from an unusually gifted and able man who has a constant struggle with psychotic parts of his personality.[4] We ended a Friday session with the patient expressing enormous relief and telling me that everything in that session had a good resonance in him. On the following Monday, he came to his session very disturbed. He said he had had a very good afternoon's work on Friday and Saturday morning, but he had had a dream on Saturday which had worried him very much. In the first part of the dream, *he was with Mrs Small. She was*

70

in bed and he was either teaching or treating her. There was also a little girl (here he became rather evasive), well, maybe a young girl. She was very pleasant with him, maybe a little sexy. And then quite suddenly someone removed a food trolley and a big cello from the room. He woke up frightened. He said it was not the first part of the dream that frightened him but the second. He felt it had something to do with a loss of internal structure. On Sunday he could still work, but he felt his work lacked depth and resonance, and he felt something was going very wrong. In the middle of Sunday night he woke up with a dream, but he could not hold on to it and instead became aware of a backache low in his back – maybe the small of his back.

He said that the Mrs Small part of the dream did not disturb him because he could quickly see through it. In the past, Mrs Small, whom he does not think much of, represented a belittling of Mrs Klein (klein = small). He understood that and supposed she represented me changed into a patient and also into a sexy little girl. He supposed it was an envious attack, because on Friday he felt so helped by me. He then had some associations to the cello – his niece had one, his admiration for Casals, and a few others – which led me to suggest tentatively that it seemed to be a very bisexual instrument. That interpretation fell rather flat. What struck him more, he said, was that it is one of the biggest musical instruments around. He then said that I had a very deep voice, and that another thing that frightened him was that when he woke up from the dream he could not remember what we were talking about in the Friday session.

It seems to me that the whole situation, which in the first night was represented by the dream, in the second night happened concretely. By changing me into Mrs Small, he had lost me as the internalized organ with deep resonance. The cello represented the mother with deep resonance, the mother who could contain the patient's projections and give a good resonance; with the loss of this organ there was an immediate concretization of the situation. On Saturday night, he belittled me, as is shown by his changing me into Mrs Small in his dream. This led to the loss of the cello – 'one of the biggest musical instruments around' – and the disappearance of the food trolley. He woke up anxious. The function of the dream to contain and elaborate anxiety began to fail. The next night, instead of a dream, he had a pain in the small of his back, a concretization of Mrs Small. Hypochondriasis, much lessened now, had at one time been a leading psychotic-flavoured symptom. The attack on the containing functions of the analyst, represented as the organ with the resonance, resulted in the patient's losing his own resonance (his depth of understanding) and his memory (he could not remember the session). When this happened, he

71

could only experience concrete physical symptoms. The belittled analyst, who in the dream was represented by Mrs Small, became a concrete pain in the small of his back.

There is a technical problem in analysing those dreams in which the dream-work is defective. It is useless in those cases to try to interpret only the content of the dreams. In recent years some analysts have expressed a certain pessimism about the usefulness of dreams in analysis. I think this is the effect of trying to analyse the content of the dream in a classical way in relation to dreams which may have to be tackled differently. In the case of Mr H, analysing the content of his dreams would make him very happy and excited, and have no therapeutic effect. Miss G would be likely to feel infinitely persecuted, taking every interpretation as a forcible pushing down her throat of her projective identifications. Mr M would experience it as our joint sexual game, with marked anti-therapeutic effect. In fact, in the beginning of his analysis with me he would get very manic and sexually excited if I started interpreting the content of his dreams. Some patients come flooding the analyst with dreams and confusion. In such a case the first thing to interpret is the flooding and the effect it is supposed to have on the analyst. Generally, in these dreams, which are primarily used for acting out in the analytic session it is this function of the dreams that has to be interpreted first of all. Only gradually, and where it connects with this function, can one address the actual content of the dream. The analyst's capacity to contain the projective identifications, under-stand, and eventually interpret them, provides a container which restores the mental space and helps to restore the symbolic function. The process described in the dream of the lost cello can be reversed. Such a restoration is shown by another patient.

After a long holiday, he lay on the couch silent and seemed very weighed down. After a long silence, he spoke inaudibly, saying the break was awful. When he got up from the couch before the holiday he felt as if he was glued to it. He felt almost paralysed. In the holiday he could not dream. He woke up feeling weighed down by stones. In the daytime he was like a zombie. From my own counter-transference experience of the heaviness of his silence, I had no doubt that those were not idle complaints, and he was projecting into me his exper-ience. Going on my past knowledge of this patient, I interpreted to him that, unable to face the separation, he glued himself to the couch and left most of himself inside me, glued to me and confused with me, so he either felt weighed down by a conglomerate of him and me, or when he cut himself off from this dreadful experience he became a zombie. He then remembered that right at the beginning of the holiday he had one nightmare in which a *huge animal, a cross between a dinosaur and a rhino, burst into a shed, bits of the shed sticking to his skin.* He woke up in fright and had not dreamed since. He associated the dinosaur to something very archaic and the rhino to nosiness, intrusion, and aggression. In the next session he said with relief that dreams had returned and he could breathe again and write again. He dreamed *of a person picking up a kitten.* He thought the kitten would be very dirty, but in fact it was not. In another dream *there was a bag of letters, like letters for Scrabble, only the bag was much bigger. He was beginning to sort them out.* Another dream (which I will not report here) dealt with separation. It seems that the experience of the previous session converted his perception of himself as a dinosaur/rhino bursting into the shed, which he breaks, and with which he gets confused (bits stuck to the skin) into that of a kitten which was not as dirty – meaning, I think, dangerous – as he thought. The kitten is picked up by a person, so I have also become more human in his perception. The jumble of letters – fragments projected into the bag – can then be sorted out to form words. (In Bion's terms, one could say that his beta elements got converted into alpha elements.) When this happens he can begin to work through the experience of separation and recover his capacity to dream.

Freud considered the understanding of dreams to be the royal road to the unconscious. As I suggested, following only the content of the dream has its limitations. If we analyse not the dream but the dreamer, and take into account the form of the dream, the way it is recounted, and the function it performs in the session, our understanding is very much enriched and we can see how the dream's function throws an important light on the functioning of the ego.

Notes

1 Mr H has been described in my 1972 paper, 'A delusional system as a defence against the re-emergence of a catastrophic situation', and in 'The function of dreams' (1981).
2 Miss G has been described in the same paper (Segal 1981).
3 This patient also is described in 'The function of dreams' (Segal 1981).
4 This patient's dream is also described in 'The function of dreams' (Segal 1981).

6

Freud and art

We laymen have always been intensely curious to know – like the Cardinal who put a similar question to Ariosto – from what sources that strange being, the creative writer, draws his material, and how he manages to make such an impression on us with it, and to arouse in us emotions of which, perhaps, we had not even thought ourselves capable.

(Freud 1908: 143)

This was the opening sentence of Freud's paper 'Creative writers and day-dreaming', which he wrote in 1907. Freud was always fascinated by art. Strachey lists no fewer than twenty-two papers of Freud dealing directly or indirectly with artists' individual works of art, themes reflected in literature, or general problems of artistic creativity. And in his books and papers references to works of art abound. This is not surprising. His research is into every manifestation of human nature and he could hardly fail to be fascinated by this uniquely human achievement. It is difficult to do full justice to the contribution which psychoanalysis has made to the understanding of art. Freud's discovery of unconscious phantasy and symbolism gave a new perspective and new depth to the understanding of the supreme symbolic expression of phantasy which is art. His contribution to aesthetics is incalculable, and it is so despite his own apparent lack of interest in aesthetics. He remarked that he was more drawn to the content of a work of art than to its form, though he understood that to the artist it was the latter that was of predominant interest.

What Freud was predominantly concerned with was the eliciting of unconscious conflicts and phantasies embodied in a work of art. Some of his papers aim at a psycho-biography of the artist, using the works of art as revealing of his inner conflicts and psychological history. In his book *Leonardo da Vinci and a Memory of his Childhood* (Freud 1910), using scant biographical data, a screen childhood memory and two of

74

his paintings, *The Mona Lisa* and *St Anne, St Mary and Jesus*, he attempts to reconstruct Leonardo's psycho-sexual development. He relates Leonardo's childhood experiences to his later conflicts between his scientific and artistic creativity. In his essay on 'Dostoevsky and parricide' (Freud 1928) through an analysis of *The Brothers Karamazov*, in the light of Dostoevsky's early experience, he illuminates the writer's personality and attempts to account for his epilepsy, gambling, and moral stance.

This approach has been criticized on many counts. (For instance, newer research suggests that it is very doubtful that Dostoevsky's father was actually murdered or that Dostoevsky believed it.) But that is in itself not important. The greatest value of these psycho-biographies has been not the restructuring of the artist's childhood, but the uncovering of phantasies expressed by the work of art. Sometimes his study of artistic work has led to new discoveries. Thus, his book on Leonardo introduced for the first time the description. of a certain form of narcissism and narcissistic object-choice. It maps out the transformation of the nipple into a penis and illustrates many other aspects of infantile psycho-sexual development. In 'Dostoevsky and parricide' Freud illustrates insights he already had into the universal theme of the Oedipus complex and parricide. But even though those are phen-omena he described before, he does derive new insights from *The Brothers. Karamazov*. For instance, he describes the splitting of the personality into many characters in the book, maybe more clearly than he had done in any clinical studies or theoretical formulations.

In other works Freud addresses himself to themes illustrating universal problems without connecting them with attempts at a direct psycho-biography of the author. For instance, in the paper 'The theme of the three caskets', he describes the relation to the three aspects of mother: the one who gives love, who becomes a partner, and who brings death. He suggests that the choice of the third casket, the leaden one, which Antonio makes in *The Merchant of Venice*, represents the choice of death. Similarly, he interprets Cordelia in *King Lear* as a symbol of death, and for him Lear's reconciliation with Cordelia is a reconciliation with death. 'Thus, man overcomes death which in thought he has acknowledged. No greater triumph of wish-fulfilment is conceivable.'

Another aspect which concerned Freud was the ability of the artist to imbue his characters with an unconscious without themselves being aware of it. Thus, in 'Delusions and dreams in Jensen's *Gradiva*' (Freud 1907), he analyses the dream of the leading character in association with that character's other activities and delusions, showing that the writer had an unconscious awareness of the dream's meaning. There is

75

an amusing example of that in his short analysis of Stefan Zweig's short story 'Four and Twenty Hours in a Woman's Life', which is an appendix to his paper on Dostoevsky (Freud 1928). The heroine of this story is a widow, and her sons grow up and no longer need her. She falls in love with a young gambler the same age as her eldest son. In his short essay, Freud is concerned with the problem of gambling and masturbation, but he relates of course the woman's passion for the young man with the loss of her son, and through that link shows the Oedipal content of the story. The amusing thing is that Stefan Zweig himself was quite unaware of the connection, of his giving the same age to the lover as to the son. He thought it was purely accidental. Nowadays, of course, we all either read Freud or at least were brought up in a culture pervaded with his ideas. A writer might have deliberately chosen such a sequence and been quite aware of the connections, but Freud shows that the intuitive, unconscious knowledge of such patterns is part of the equipment of the artist. The writer brought in this detail of the young man's age because it felt intuitively, artistically right.

In most of Freud's writings the actual problem of artistic creativity is touched on only tangentially, but it is touched on. For instance, in *Leonardo da Vinci* he contends that in the smile of the Gioconda Leonardo revives the expression of his mother's smile; and that in *St Anne, St Mary and Jesus* he aims at integrating his mother and step-mother; this is also reflected in the formal aspect of the painting – its pyramidal form. But mostly, with typical modesty, Freud disclaims that he has any light to throw either on the nature of the artistic gift or the artistic merits of work; yet he is drawn to the problem again and again.

He sometimes speaks of the mystery of artistic achievement. In the paper 'Creative writers and day-dreaming' (Freud 1908), he tackles the mystery more directly. (I am not happy with this new translation of Freud's original title, 'Der Dichter'. The older translation was 'The poet and his relation to day-dreaming'. I think the nearest equivalent we could find is the Scottish 'The maker'.) In that paper he compares and contrasts the creative writer (and it would hold in his view of all artists) with the day-dreamer. The background to the understanding of this paper is Freud's concept of the pleasure–pain principle and the reality principle. When the reality principle is established, says Freud, one mode of mental functioning remains split off from this development, and that is phantasy. In this formulation Freud sometimes leaves it unclear whether he means deep, unconscious phantasying or conscious fantasying. In this paper he approaches the problem, to begin with, from the angle of conscious fantasy – day-dreaming.

The day-dreamer in his day-dream ignores reality and gives rein to his pleasure-pain principle in evolving wishful phantasies. The artist has this in common with the day-dreamer – that he creates a world of phantasy in which he can fulfil his unconscious wishes. In one important way, however, he differs from the day-dreamer in that he finds a way back to reality in his artistic creation, and in that way his work is more akin to children's play, in that the children in their play use and mould their external world to their wishes. Freud makes it clear that he contrasts play not with the serious – play can be very serious to the child – but with the real. In his play the child creates a world which he knows is not real. Like the child in his play, the artist creates a fantasy world which he knows is not real, or rather, I would say, that it is real only in a certain sense. It does have a reality of its own, different from what we commonly call 'real'.

But what is it, Freud asks, that makes us enjoy this fantasy world, those day-dreams of the poet? The wishes expressed in the work of art are repressed wishes, unacceptable to consciousness. What makes us accept their expression by the artist? Freud gives a threefold answer. First, the writer's phantasy must lose its purely egocentric character and touch on something universal. Second, the wish is partly disguised. It may be softened and it is disguised in ways similar to the disguises of the dream. And third, the artist gives us the aesthetic pleasure which diverts us from the hidden thought – a pleasure which bribes us to accept the hidden thought. He compares the aesthetic pleasure to the fore-pleasure in sex.

> We give the name of an *incentive bonus* or a *fore-pleasure*, to a yield of pleasure such as this, which is offered to us so as to make possible the release of still greater pleasure arising from deeper psychical sources.
> (Freud 1908: 153)

But by what means this is achieved is a question which he confesses baffles him. The nearest he came to tackling the question of means (as he himself noticed) was in fact in his book *Jokes and their Relation to the Unconscious* (Freud 1905), where he describes certain mechanisms to achieve what he called 'pleasurable release from inhibition' (Wollheim 1973).

One could say that Freud, in describing the aesthetic satisfaction as no more than a bribe, a kind of wrapping for the real, instinctual satisfaction, makes light of the aesthetic experience itself. And on this point he was open to criticism.

In 1924, in the British Psychological Society, Roger Fry read a paper entitled 'The artist and psychoanalysis'. I know that since then many more erudite works on Freud's approach have been written on that topic, but I want to concentrate on this one because it seems to me to go to the heart of the matter. I consider it still the best statement of the recurring criticism that the psychoanalytic approach to art is reductive. Both those elements in which Fry is right in his critique of Freud, and in those in which he is wrong, are worth considering – also, I must admit, because Clive Bell's notion of the significant form espoused also by Fry is one which, in some ways, is congenial to me, and some of their statements are illuminating and consistent with the psycho-analytical view. I shall return to them in the next chapter.

Fry criticizes Freud under three main headings. First, and maybe the most important, he questions the idea of wish-fulfilment. He draws attention to the fact that Freud, in his paper on 'Creative writers and day-dreaming', takes as his example the popular novelette which embodies and fulfils superficial sexual or ambitious wishes, and points out that this precisely is not art. His second objection is that Freud concentrates on the content, whereas the essence of art is its form. And, third, he objects to the idea of symbolism in art.

What Freud describes as the emotions aroused by art are what Fry and Bell call 'associative emotions', not the aesthetic emotion proper. A work of art can give rise to any number of emotions, some of which Bell called associative. For instance, one may be moved by a tune because one first heard it when meeting a lover; or one can be moved by one's national anthem because of one's patriotism. I think that Freud's idea that we identify with a successful hero in a work of art, but also in a cheap novelette, would belong, partly at least, to the associ-ative emotions. But there exists a particular emotion independent of those, which is the aesthetic experience. Bell, speaking of visual arts, says that

There is a particular kind of emotion provoked by works of visual art, and that this emotion is provoked by every kind of visual art, by pictures, sculpture, buildings, etc., is not disputed I think by anyone capable of feeling it. This emotion is called the aesthetic emotion; and if we can discover some quality common and peculiar to all the objects that provoke it, we shall have solved what I take to be the central problem of aesthetics. We shall have discovered the essential quality in a work of art that distinguishes a work of art from all other classes of objects.

This essential quality which he postulated Bell called the significant form.

These relations and combinations of lines and colours, these aesthetic lines and forms I call significant form, and significant form is the one quality common to all visual works of art.

(Bell 1914)

And though Bell speaks of visual arts only, this obviously can be extended to other arts as well – music in particular, with its lack of verbalizable content. The nature of this aesthetic pleasure is not easy to define, but Fry says it does not depend on libidinal wish-fulfilment, but rather on the recognition of inevitable sequences.

The pleasure which consists in the recognition of inevitable sequences, a pleasure which you see corresponds to the pleasure we find in marking the inevitable sequence of the notes in a tune; in fact again a pleasure derived from the contemplation of the relations and correspondences of form.

(Fry 1924)

There is also something objective and disinterested in the aesthetic emotion and something akin, Fry says, to the search for truth by the scientist. This criticism of Freud is partly valid. Art has similarities to the child's play and to the day-dreamer and to the dreamer, but it is none of those things.

Fry, however, does less than justice to Freud in his over-simplification of the idea of wish-fulfilment, but in a way Freud, too, does not do himself justice in this particular paper. In other later papers – for instance, in his discussion of Michaelangelo's *Moses* – he lays much more stress on the unconscious conflict, but it must be remembered, as Professor Wollheim emphasizes in his papers on Freud's aesthetics (Wollheim 1973), that nearly all of Freud's papers on art precede his structural theory of mind; and that he did not apply his new insights to his theoretical statements on art. For instance, his notion of working through an unconscious conflict would have enabled him to think of art as work rather than day-dreaming or play. Also it would illuminate the question of the so-called wish-fulfilment, because the question would be, also, which wish is fulfilled – that of the id, the ego, or the superego, the aggressive or the libidinal?

In his 1908 paper, Freud speaks of an unconscious wish and repression, but in the essay on Dostoevsky (Freud 1928) he makes it clear that the work of art has to reconcile the contradictory aims of the id and the superego. If there is wish-fulfilment in art – and there must be, since there is wish-fulfilment in all human activities – it is not a simple omnipotent wish-fulfilment of a libidinal or aggressive wish. It is a fulfilment of the wish to work through a problem in a particular way, not what is understood by wish-fulfilment, namely, omnipotence.

79

Most of Freud's writing on art precedes his conceptualization of the unconscious ego (that part of the unconscious which elaborates and works through conflicts). The work of art is, I think, an expression of this working through. The nature of the psychic conflict and the way the artist tries to resolve it in his unconscious ego may throw light on the significant form. This will be the theme of my next chapter.

Also, the content and the form and the associative and the purely aesthetic emotion cannot really be separated without impoverishing the aesthetic experience. For instance, Picasso's *Guernica* made a calculated, strong appeal to all emotions stirred by the bombing of Guernica. We cannot separate the associative emotions of that kind from the aesthetic merit. There is a path leading from the immediate associative emotion: the Spanish war to all war, as in Goya's black paintings. Those emotions, unlike the incidental associative emotions, are universal, and, consciously or unconsciously, the artist aims at evoking them. And in a work of art the path leads not only from the current war to war in general, but also to what such wars represent in our unconscious. For instance, the head of the dying horse in Picasso's paintings probably awakens the earliest phantasies of oral sadism with the experience of being both the aggressor and the aggressed. The horse is a dying victim, yet it is his enormous teeth that stand out, symbolizing, I think, its own, and our own, oral aggression. The broken lines, the fragmentary presentation of the human and animal figures, also correspond to unconscious phantasies of fragmented objects, victims of sadism. The power of the impact is due to Picasso's capacity to mobilize, via the associative emotions, deeper unconscious ones. And this makes the work live long past the actual events associated with it in our minds. Similarly, love poems (for instance) can arouse strong associative emotions to one's own experience as a lover, but the poem reaches deeper than that.

Abstract artists on the other hand, try to avoid all associative emotions, but they too only succeed by pure form if they can express some deeper unconscious emotions. If they fail in that their work becomes purely decorative and, though it can give pleasure, fails to arouse deep aesthetic emotions.

Indeed, in some way, Fry and Bell do acknowledge this. Fry, at the conclusion of his paper, says:

It looks as though art had got access to the substratum of all the emotional colours of life, to something that underlies all the particular and specialised emotions of actual life. It seems to derive an emotional energy from the very conditions of our existence by its revelation of an emotional existence in time and space, though it may be that art really calls up, as it were, the residual traces left on the spirit by the different emotions of life without, however, recalling the actual experiences, so that we get an echo of the emotion without the limitation and particular direction which it had in experience.

(Fry 1924)

When Freud compares the form in art with fore-pleasure he wonders what the primary pleasure is. I think that primary pleasure is not, as Freud sometimes thought, or, as is the case in wit, a pleasurable release of inhibition, but is in fact the aesthetic pleasure proper itself. And, significantly, in one of those illuminating asides, Freud threw light on the subject of form. At a meeting of the Vienna Psychoanalytic Society in 1909, he noted that 'A content has, as a rule, its history, and that with regard to art one could properly say that art form is a precipitate of an older content'.

And to understand this precipitate, the notion of unconscious symbolism is crucial. Bell and Fry themselves do not tell us enough about the significant form, what makes it significant? It is not sufficient to say that it is a particular combination of lines and forms.

Fry says: 'In proportion, as the artist is pure, he is opposed to all symbolism.' But he refers here to conscious symbolism, which was a particular *bête noire* of the formalist school. He has no understanding of true, dynamic, unconscious symbolism. I think that form, be it musical, visual, or verbal, can move us so deeply because it symbolically embodies an unconscious meaning. In other words, art embodies and symbolizes and evokes in the recipient a certain kind of archaic emotion of a preverbal kind.

Bell quotes, with approval, Mallarmé's comment on Gautier: 'He banished the dream, which is the first thing a poet has to do.' Proust makes Elstir, the painter, say the opposite: 'If a little dream is dangerous, the cure for it is not less dreaming, but more dream – the whole dream.' Which of those sayings, sounding so convincing, is the true one? I think it depends on what you mean by 'dream'. If by 'dream' you mean a wish-fulfilling phantasy based on the denial of internal and external realities, then surely Mallarmé is right. But if by dream you mean imagination – getting in touch as deeply and truthfully as you can with the contents of your own mind – then Elstir is right. It is in the depths of his dream, his unconscious phantasy life, that the poet finds his inspiration.

In his later work – for instance, in the *New Introductory Lectures* – Freud (1933) makes it clear that art is rooted in deep, unconscious phantasy. And he suggests that in the artist there is a certain degree of laxity of repression which is decisive for allowing the expression of phantasy. He weakens his case, however, when he returns to formulations similar to the ones in 'Creative writers and day-dreaming, when he speaks of the artist's relation to reality. He says that the writer fails in reality and turns to phantasy but that he returns to reality through his work, which then brings him what he seeks, 'honour, power and the love of women'. This is a kind of formulation which leaves Freud open to attack, since it is well known that true artists often sacrifice money, power, position, and possibly love of women, for the sake of the integrity of their art. As indeed Freud himself did, jeopardizing his career, attracting opprobium, for the sake of the truth which he felt he had discovered.

And here we have to come back to the pleasure principle and the reality principle. An artist does not operate mainly, as Freud originally thought, on the pleasure principle. Freud says the artist finds a way back to reality, but I think the artist, in some essential way, never departs from reality. I agree with Bell that the essence of the aesthetic experience has something to do with such feelings as inevitability and truth, which is the opposite of the omnipotent wish-fulfilment. The truth that the artist is after is primarily psychic truth. And it is Freud, of course, who has taught us the importance of psychic reality.

In that the artist differs essentially from the day-dreamer. Where the day-dreamer avoids conflict by a phantasy of omnipotent wish-fulfilment and a denial of external and psychic realities, the artist seeks to locate his conflict and resolve it in his creation. He does not look for easy solutions. But Freud himself was an artist, and, I think, knew far more about art and the aesthetic experience than he gave himself credit for, and than he encompasses in his theoretical formulations about art. His paper on Michaelangelo's *Moses* is quite striking in that respect. He gives a careful analysis of the position of Moses' beard and his right hand, and the tables this hand is supposed to hold. And from this analysis he deduces the previous movement: 'The loop of the beard would thus be an intimation of the path taken by this hand. . . . And this new position, which can only be understood with reference to the former one, is now retained.'

And about the tables: 'We begin to suspect that the tables too have arrived at their present position as a result of the previous movement.'

This careful analysis of the sculpture shows that its dynamism is due to the unnatural position of the beard, hand, and tables, in that way conveying the translation from one state of mind to another.

Let us compare this with Rodin's description of movement. In his dialogue with Paul Gsell, Rodin (1911) explains why a photograph, however well taken, of a body in motion appears immobile. It is

because it portrays only one moment of the movement and is fixed
there. In a sculpture the position of limbs is in fact unnatural because it
contains remnants of the previous position. He shows that his *St John*,
which appears strongly to be walking, has both feet on the ground.
Had a photograph been taken of a walker in a similar position his back
foot would already have been lifted. And he demonstrated it on a
number of other sculptures. His analysis of the leg position parallels that
of Freud's analysis of the position of Moses' hand. Thus, what Freud
works out as the 'secret' of the dynamism of the seated figure is in fact,
at least according to Rodin, a general aesthetic law. What Freud
describes is 'the means' by which the artist achieves his effect. He sees
in Michaelangelo's *Moses* a great man overcoming a great wrath. This
emotion is expressed by a movement. Rodin, in his *Dialogue*, also
emphasizes that emotion is expressed by movement. Other analyses by
Rodin also come close to Freud's. He comments on the nature of the
resemblance of a bust to the model. He says the photograph is never a
true resemblance the way a bust is, because it touches only the surface
and is only the impression of the moment, whilst the bust can convey
from various angles different emotions and the transitions between
them. Rodin also implies that he portrays attitudes and emotions of
which the model is unconscious. Sitters, according to him, almost
invariably dislike busts made by real sculptors because they show
aspects of their personality which they do not know or do not want to
know about. This comment of Rodin's applies, however, not only to
busts with a model. It is quite clear that his imaginary figures are
imbued with the same life on the same principles. Like characters in a
great book, they are also endowed with an unconscious. I find it
fascinating how close Freud's understanding, particularly maybe as
shown in Michaelangelo's *Moses*', comes to the views of one of the
greatest sculptors and teachers of art.

And it is in this paper that Freud came closest, I think, to touching
on the aesthetic experience.

> In my opinion what grips us so powerfully can only be the artist's
> *intention* in so far as he succeeds in expressing it in his work and in
> getting us to understand it. I realize that this cannot be merely a
> matter of *intellectual* comprehension; what he aims at is to awaken in
> us the same emotional attitude, the same mental constellation which
> produces in him the impetus to create.
>
> (Freud 1914: 212)

This I think is a most original and profound statement, rarely recognized and quoted.

Another great artist expresses a similar insight. Shelley, in a note-book, writes:

> If it were possible that a person should give a faithful history of his being from the earliest epochs of his recollection, a picture would be presented such as the world has never contemplated before. A mirror would be held up to all men in which they might behold their own recollections and, in dim perspective, their shadowy hopes and fears – all that they dare not, or that daring and desiring, they could not expose to the open eyes of day. But thought can with difficulty visit the intricate and winding chambers which it inhabits.
> (Shelley 1812)

But Freud found himself puzzled by the double problem 'from what sources that strange being, the creative writer, draws his material' (Freud 1908); that is, what is that constellation and the unconscious intention, and how does he 'manage to make such an impression on us with it'? Freud was aware that this is a crucial question and he does not pretend to know the answer.

7

Art and the depressive position

Melanie Klein's first paper on art, 'Infantile anxiety situations reflected in a work of art and the creative impulse' (1929), addresses itself to the sources of the creative impulse. In that paper Klein discusses first a libretto by Colette for a Ravel opera, *L'Enfant et les Sortilèges*. In that libretto a little boy in a fit of temper attacks various objects in his room and attempts to hurt a squirrel. The objects come alive and they, as well as little animals, grow to enormous proportions and attack the child. At some point in the mêlée a little squirrel gets hurt and falls to the ground. On an impulse of compassion the little boy picks up the squirrel. Immediately the scene changes. Objects and animals become friendly and the little boy calls 'Maman', and some of the objects and animals echo him. Klein uses this example to describe what she then considered a leading anxiety in little boys, related to their phantasy attacks on the mother's body and the paternal penis within it, and shows how the persecutory anxiety to which it gives rise gets modified by reparation.

The second example is taken from a biography of a Swedish painter, Ruth Kjär. That young woman suffered from recurring depressions in which she felt invaded by an empty space inside her. One day a picture which she had on loan had been taken back by the painter and she could not stand the empty space on the wall. Her biographer says: 'On the wall there was an empty space which in some inexplicable way seemed to coincide with the empty space within her....The empty space grinned hideously down on her.'

The intolerability of the empty space, according to the biographer, compelled her to do a painting herself. And this was the beginning of a successful career as a painter.

One of her early pictures represented a wrinkled old woman in a state of disconsolate resignation. One of the last pictures was a portrait of her mother when young and beautiful. She has the effect of a 'magnificent woman of primitive times'. The biographer comments, 'The blank space has been filled.'

Melanie Klein uses this example, like the previous one, to refer to some basic anxieties, this time in a girl. And again she emphasizes the role of reparation as represented by the two pictures singled out by a perceptive biographer. But in this second example, Klein makes a direct link between this need for reparation and the origin of the creative impulse.

What Klein says about Ruth Kjär seems to echo what Fry said of Cézanne. In his introduction to the First Post-Impressionist Exhibition in England, he said that his aim 'was not to paint attractive pictures but to work out his salvation'. Klein's paper, written in 1929, precedes her major work on the depressive position. But what she shows in the change of the boy's experience in Colette's libretto is what she would later describe as the shift from a paranoid to a depressive position. It is interesting to me that this is the paper which immediately precedes that on symbol-formation, symbol-formation to my mind being the very essence of artistic creativity.

In 1952, in my paper 'A psycho-analytic approach to aesthetics', I put forward the suggestion that the artistic impulse is specifically related to the depressive position. The artist's need is to recreate what he feels in the depth of his internal world.

It is his inner perception of the deepest feeling of the depressive position that his internal world is shattered which leads to the necessity for the artist to recreate something that is felt to be a whole new world. This is what every major artist does – creates a world. When we read an impressive novel, or look at a painting, or listen to music, we are drawn into a complete new world. And it is a world of its own. However realistic the painter or the writer may be, two painters painting the same landscape, or the same portrait, or two novelists describing the same society, in fact create worlds of their own. Shelley says:

And dream
Of waves, flowers, clouds, woods, rocks, and all that we
Read in their smiles and call reality.

This world has traces of a world one has known.

Proust's major work, *A la Recherche du Temps Perdu* (1908-12), contains an insightful description of the actual process of creating. He describes it thus:

Il fallait ... faire sortir de la pénombre ce que j'avais senti, de le

reconvertir en un équivalent spirituel. Or ce moyen qui me paraissait le seul qu'était-ce autre chose que de créer une oeuvre d'art?
(*I had to recapture from the shade that which I had felt, to reconvert it into its psychic equivalent. But the way to do it, the only one I could see, what was it – but to create a work of art?*)

And he recalls his dead or otherwise lost loved objects:

Et certes il n'y aurait pas qu'Albertine, que ma grandmère, mais bien d'autres encore dont j'aurais pu assimiler une parole, un regard, mais en tant que créatures individuelles je ne m'en rappellais plus; un livre est un grand cimetière où sur la plupart des tombes on ne peut plus lire les noms éffacés.

(*And indeed it was not only Albertine, not only my grandmother, but many others still from whom I might well have assimilated a gesture or a word, but whom I could not even remember as distinct persons; a book is a vast graveyard whereon most of the tombstones one can read no more the faded names.*)

He also indicates that the people in his graveyard are part of his unconscious. One can no more read (remember) distinctly the names. And he emphasizes that it is only the fact that these objects and the past are lost that gives an impetus and the need to recreate them. 'On ne peut recréer ce qu'on aime qu'en le renonçant' ('*It is only when we have renounced it that we can recreate what we love*'), says Elstir, the painter, to the narrator.

Proust also emphasizes that the only way he can do it is by finding a symbolic expression: art is essentially a search for a symbolic expression. The creation of this inner world, I contend, is unconsciously also a recreation of a lost world. This is explicitly stated by Proust. Many other artists have expressed this too. In *The Prelude*, Wordsworth describes similar feelings of loss and regaining, and he says, referring to his childhood experiences:

How strange that all the terrors, pains, and early miseries,
Regrets, vexations, lassitudes interfused
Within my mind, should e'er have borne a part,
And that a needful part, in making up
The calm existence that is mine when I
Am worthy of myself!

(*The Prelude*, Book I, Lines 344–50)

This passage follows the description of plundering a nest, so regrets in this passage also include guilt.

Other artists are often not aware of the nature of their creative impulse. Joseph Conrad, for instance, in his *Some Reminiscences* (1912; US title, *A Personal Record*), said that he had no idea whence came his impulse to write. He emerged in his mid-thirties as a completely mature artist, with no juvenilia, no early attempts at writing. He even hated writing letters. But there are two short stories of his which I think can throw some light on his emergence as a writer. They are 'The secret sharer' (Conrad 1912b) and 'The shadow-line' (Conrad 1917). The two stories were written at different times and belong to different collections, but they refer to the same period in Conrad's life; namely, the period of his first command (in fact, the first title of 'The shadow line' was 'First command'), that is, the time shortly preceding Conrad's beginning as a writer. They have other similarities. Conrad himself mentions that they are the two stories of calm water which he contrasts with his two stories of storm – *The Nigger of the 'Narcissus'* (1897) and *Typhoon* (1903). Also, in each, the hero has a double. Each is dominated by the island of Koh-ring: 'The island of Koh-ring – a great black upheaved ridge amongst a lot of tiny islets lying upon the glassy water like a Triton amongst minnows seemed to be the centre of the fatal circle.' The third story, also pertinent, is *The Heart of Darkness* (1902). That refers to the Congo where Conrad nearly lost his un-completed manuscript.

In the first story, the 'secret sharer' is the captain's double, who had committed a murder. In 'Shadow Line', a ship is becalmed immediately after leaving port. All the crew come down with fever. The first mate is demented and convinced that the ship is haunted by the ghost of the previous captain, whom he hates and wished dead. The ship is becalmed and the young captain feels a total responsibility for the ship and the life of his men. The deadly calm, the dying men, the feeling of being haunted by a vengeful ghost of a dead parent, the captain's feeling of total and solitary responsibility to bring life to his dying ship and men is a marvellous picture of depression and the captain's heroic struggle against it. The ship eventually reaches port, and the captain psychically survives this ordeal, emerging more mature. He has crossed the shadow line between youth and manhood. That this external situation expresses also an internal state of mind is shown by the captain's double, the steward of the ship. The steward of the same age and type of personality as the captain is the only other member of the crew not ill with fever, but he has a fatal disease of the heart. As the ship reaches port safely the steward signs off, confessing his terrible fear of death, and leaves the ship carrying the pain and the death in his heart. The captain had reached the depths of despair when he discovered that there was no quinine on board and felt it was his fault because he had not checked it. It is at this moment that, to save himself from madness, he starts writing a diary. He wrote 'to work out his salvation'.

And it is while he was coping with his first command, and, according to his letter, in the throes of depression, that Conrad started writing.

Proust's Elstir cries out 'One can only create what one has renounced'; this is consistent with some of Freud's views on sublimation, when he emphasized the need of inhibiting the instinctual aim – a renunciation. From the point of view of object relations such a renunciation would entail the renunciation of the possession of an object. Freud also says that we cannot give up an object without internalizing it. This internalization makes the object part of psychic reality, the reality which the artist has to represent. In *The Moses of Michelangelo*, Freud (1914: 212), stated that what the artist aims to reproduce in his work is 'the same mental constellation as that which produces in him the impetus to create'. If this is the mental constellation he manages to make us identify with and re-live, it would explain the depths of the satisfaction and the quality of uplift that any aesthetic experience gives us; it enables us to participate in a creative act.

While Freud found inspiration in and could analyse the broad phantasies, particularly the Oedipal myth, in works of art, he found himself baffled by two problems: that of the nature of the creative impulse and that of the means by which the artist captures and engages his audience. I think the two are in fact connected. Of course every artist has his own individual technique and his own particular problems and emotions. And at different times in different works he expresses various facets of his experience. But are there some common factors which are essential to evoke in us an experience which makes us class certain products, otherwise so different from each other, as art? What is the 'significant form' which applies equally to music, writing, painting, and other arts? This of course is the field of the historian of art or the philosopher of aesthetics. Nevertheless, I think that Freud's idea that the artist aims at evoking in the recipient of his art the same constellation of unconscious feeling which motivated him suggests that the emotions must have something in common to arouse the emotion called 'aesthetic experience'. And if I am right in thinking that the specific constellation that is aimed at in depth has to do with an attempted resolution of a depressive conflict, including its early Oedipal constellation, then the means must be such as to convey both the conflict and the reparative attempt at resolution.

And I think here that the aesthetic categories 'beautiful' and 'ugly' are of help to us. Beauty is usually described as having to do with harmony, rhythm, wholeness. Fry, in the address I quoted, often speaks of harmony. Herbert Read says that what we find beautiful and rhythmical are simple arithmetic proportions which correspond to the way we are built and our bodies work.

Two British psychoanalytic writers address themselves seriously to the particular problem of ugliness and beauty. Rickman, in 'On the nature of ugliness and the creative impulses' (1940), and Ella Sharpe, 'Certain aspects of sublimation and delusion' (1930). For Ella Sharpe, 'ugly' means destroyed, arrhythmic, and connected with painful tension; beauty she considers essentially as rhythm, and equates it with the experiences of goodness in rhythmic sucking, satisfactory defecation, and sexual intercourse. Rickman equates beautiful with the whole object and the ugly with the fragmented, destroyed one. And he says that we recoil from the ugly. However, these authors equate 'beautiful' with aesthetically satisfying. This cannot be so. If that were the case nothing would be more beautiful than a circle or a rhythmical drumbeat. The aesthetic experience is in my view a particular combination of what has been called 'ugly' and what could be called 'beautiful'.

Rodin says:

What we call 'ugly' in reality, in art can become great beauty. We call 'ugly' that which is formless, unhealthy, which suggests illness, suffering, destruction, which is contrary to regularity – the sign of health.... We also call ugly the immoral, the vicious, the criminal and all abnormality which brings evil – the soul of parricide, the traitor, the self-seeker... But let a great artist get hold of this ugliness; immediately he transfigures it – with a touch of his magic wand he makes it into beauty.

(Rodin 1911)

In my 1952 paper I take as a paradigm of creativity the classical tragedy. One could say that there the ugly is largely in the content. It presents what Rodin called ugly, including emotionally ugly – hubris, treachery, parricide, matricide – and the inevitable destruction and death of the participants. There is an unflinching facing of the forces of destruction; and there is beauty in the feeling of inner consistency and psychological truth in the depiction of those destructive forces of conflict and their inevitable outcome. There is also a counterbalancing of the violence by its opposite in the form: the rhythm of the poetry and the Aristotelian unities give a harmonious and particularly strictly ordered form. This form contains feelings which otherwise might be uncontainable. It is the magic wand of poetry

90

which Rodin speaks of that transforms the ugliness into beauty, though I do not quite agree that this is a 'magic wand' at work. It is the artist's work which produces the transformation.

Speaking of tragedy, of course I made a quite arbitrary distinction between the content and form, because the same conflict can be expressed in form itself, or in any combination of form and content. In tragedy it is mainly the content that represents aggression and the internal disaster, and form which restores a harmonious world. In cubist art the 'ugly' is in the breaking up of form itself – the beautiful in its reconstruction in a new form.

For the expression of this conflict in form, as well as content, Picasso is an interesting example. When Picasso visited Madrid at the age of nineteen he went into a deep depression which lasted about a year. This seems to have been stimulated by seeing real great art which he felt he could not emulate, particularly Velázquez. In old age he painted the magnificent *Las Meninas*, in which he fragmented, dismantled, and then reconstructed in his own way the painting of Velázquez. It is as though it took him nearly a lifetime to reconstruct what in his mind he wanted to break up, or had broken up inside himself in his depression at the age of nineteen. When he attempted this reconstruction he produced a work as original and immortal as Velázquez himself. Here the content of the picture, children playing, is cheerful, and the resolution of destruction and restoration is expressed in the form.

In the previous chapter, I spoke of the painting *Guernica*. That is also a beautiful example of the process, I think, underlying creativity. *Guernica* is a picture of utter destruction and desolation. What makes it different from a photographic record of the horrors? If we look at the details there are some contrasts within the general destruction of the scene. In the upper left-hand corner there is the head of a bull, giving the impression of extraordinary detachment and serenity. On the right-hand side, paralleling it, the head of a woman looking on with a kind of detached compassion – a transformation of the Marseillaise of Rude into a mourning, compassionate figure. The formal elements seem balanced in an almost Leonardo-like way. In the first sketches of *Guernica*, Picasso mapped out a triangle, into which he fitted only lights and shadows. The shattered elements, the broken-up limbs are composed into formal wholes. In the book on this painting, *Picasso's Guernica – Genesis of a Painting*, Rudolf Arnheim traces the stages of development of the painting from the early sketches to the final form. At some point he says:

At the time sketch one was made, the total concept consisted essentially of four very simple and relatively independent elements –

91

the upright figure of the bull; the upside down corpse of the horse; the horizontal pointer of the light bearing woman and the inarticulate spread of the bodies on the ground. In the later sketches the growth of connections can be demonstrated: in No. 6 the horse responds to the theme of the light. In No. 10 the bull does the same and the horse now communicates with the warrior. Thus, groupings begin to form. But these groups at first are as isolated as the individual figures were at the beginning. No.12 is found to be made up of three fairly simple clusters: the bull, the horse and the warrior, the mother with her child. In No. 15 a tangle of insufficiently co-ordinated appeals seems to fill the picture. In the early states of the mural itself, the central triangle of the victims has, at first, no commerce with the group of the bull. Only when the horse's head is raised and turned leftward, and when the warrior's head is made to address the bull, a connection between the two groups is established.

Note the recurring theme: 'growth of connections can be demonstrated'; 'the horse now communicates with the warrior'; 'groupings begin to form'; 'a connection between the two groups is established'. In other words, there is a constant work of integration establishing connections, creating formal wholes, finding a rhythm. There is also an uplift – contrasting with the horror of the scene there is an upward lift of light towards the centre right, giving a feeling similar to that of a Gothic cathedral.

The ugliness of the breaking up and devastation is transformed into an object of beauty. The magic transformation Rodin spoke of is achieved by a process of integration.

True reparation, in contrast to manic reparation, must include an acknowledgement of aggression and its effect. And there can be no art without aggression. In parables about creativity, like Golding's *The Spire* (1964), or Patrick White's *The Vivisector* (White 1970), the theme of destroying and re-creating recur continually. Jocelyn, the hero of *The Spire* exclaims 'How many dead are built into our towers!' and also 'There is no innocent art'. The painter/hero of *The Vivisector*, when asked why he painted a particularly cruel portrait, says, 'To atone for some of my enormities'. He also says, 'I was born with knives in my eyes and my hands.'

It is significant for me that the paper in which Freud comes closest to tackling an aesthetic problem, the *The Moses of Michelangelo*, he thinks that the experience conveyed is that of overcoming wrath, contempt, and despair.

Adrian Stokes, in *The Invitation in Art* (1965), describes vividly the first step in starting artistic work as containing aggression. The marble has to be cut and hammered; clay has to be pummelled. He describes the painter's anxiety before putting the first line or blob of paint on to a virgin canvas; the writer's anxiety in facing the virgin page. Once the first line has been written or drawn something flawless has been infringed and it has to be made good.

It could be argued that what I say applies to tragedy or romantic art and that my thesis itself has a romantic bias to it. Would it apply, for instance, to classical art – perfect, beautiful shapes, showing no destruction and no flaws? I think it would.

Rilke said, 'Beauty is the beginning of terror that we are just able to bear.' Goethe, after an early romantic phase, became increasingly classical. In the second part of *Faust*, Faust wants to put on a magic show of Helen and Paris; and he needs to create what is to him the perfect classic beauty, Helen. Mephistopheles sends him to the Mothers; they are so terrifying that even Mephistopheles dare not speak of them, warning Faust that he will have to face unnamed terrors to go where there is no road:

Kein Weg! Ins Unbetretene
Nicht zu Betretende; ein Weg ans Unerbetene,
Nicht zu Erbittende.

He must face endless emptiness:

Nichts Wirst du sehn in ewig leerer Ferne,
Den Schritt nicht hören den du tust,
Nichts Festes finden, wo du ruhst.

It is also significant that great Greek art, in contrast to imitations, never actually keeps to perfect proportions. There are always some 'flaws' which are essential to make the work feel alive. Nietzsche said, in relation to Greek art, that there is no great art without tension. The tension that Nietzsche speaks of must be maintained to the last moment. However cheerful and serene the work, it conveys to the recipient's unconscious a tension that underlies the creative process. Nietzsche said that it is Greek art (that is, 'classic art') which has taught us that there are no truly beautiful surfaces without dreadful depths. And he speaks here of classical art *par excellence*.

Klee is to my mind a particularly serene and in some ways cheerful painter. This is what he says: 'To achieve vital harmony the picture must be constructed of parts themselves incomplete brought into harmony at the last stroke' – this from a most gentle and serene painter (Klee 1908). Furthermore, I think the resolution is never quite complete. We must complete the work internally. Our own imaginations must bridge the last gap. (Anton Ehrenzweig [1948] draws attention to the fact that a drawing is made always with interrupted lines.) Hence, I think, the feeling of inexhaustibility – we can look at a picture, or listen to a piece of music, read poetry again and again. We do not exhaust the possibilities of completion. Inferior art gives us, as it were, all the answers. Once we have seen, or heard, or read, we may enjoy the experience, but have no wish to repeat it.

The artist's reparative work is never completed. Picasso remarked that a picture is never finished. One has to know when to stop and say the rest in the next one. Furthermore, the finished product bears traces of this incompletion.

In brief, the link I see between creative impulse and the means of evoking the aesthetic emotion is this. The act of creation at depth has to do with an unconscious memory of a harmonious internal world and the experience of its destruction; that is, the depressive position. The impulse is to recover and recreate this lost world. The means to achieve it has to do with the balance of 'ugly' elements with beautiful elements in such a way as to evoke an identification with this process in the recipient. Aesthetic experience in the recipient involves psychic work. This is what distinguishes it from pure entertainment or sensuous pleasure. And we know that people vary in their capacity to accomplish such work. Not only does the recipient identify with the creator, thereby reaching deeper feelings than he could do by himself; he also feels that it is left to him to look for completion.

It has been argued against my point of view that the artist does not recreate, he creates; a work of art has to be and always is original. This is true. That the actual work of art is original and the artist aims, though not always, at originality, does not mean that it cannot in the unconscious be felt as a recreation. In Chapter 2, I discuss a patient who dreamed of putting together a jigsaw which represented putting together her shattered internal family. The actual book she was writing had nothing to do with her or any other family. It was the act of putting the book together that held the unconscious meaning of restoring something in herself. What is restored is an internal reality, as in Wordsworth's saying, in *The Prelude* 'what we call reality'. And everyone restores his own individual reality.

There is also often a feeling, both in the artist and in the recipient, that the artist not so much creates but reveals a reality. It has been said that nobody noticed the mists on the Thames till Turner painted them. If a painting is of a landscape known to us we feel that aspects, features, feelings have been revealed which we never noticed before. Books reveal to us another aspect of reality. I think the feeling of truth and inevitability that Fry describes as part of the aesthetic experience has to do with a feeling of revelation of some half-perceived, apprehended truth, which is discovered, not invented.

It is a paradox that the artist's work is new and yet arises from an urge to recreate or restore. This paradox is inherent in symbolism.

Another aspect of the artist's creation being something new, though it originates in the phantasy of a recreation, is the role of symbolism. The work of art is often felt by the artist as a symbolic baby. In that sense also it is felt as something new. All reparative activity has a symbolic element. What is unique about artistic creativity is that the whole reparative act is in the creation of the symbol. In Proust's words: 'But the way to do it, the only way I could see, what was it but to create a work of art.'

In Chapter 3, on symbolism, I emphasize that in the symbol-formation that is developed in the depressive position the symbol is not equated with the object; it is the result of the psychic work of the subject, and therefore the subject has the freedom of its use. The symbol is not a copy of the object – it is something created anew. The world the artist creates is created anew. This too has to do with a reparative reconstruction. It is a restoring in one's internal world of a parental couple creating a new baby. I found it very moving in analysing a certain inhibited artist to see the shift from a narcissistic position, in which the artistic product is put forward as self-created faeces, with a constant terror that one's product will be revealed as shit, to the genital position in which the creation is felt to be a baby resulting from meaningful internal intercourse. And the work of art is then felt as having a life of its own and one which will survive the artist.

This symbolic recreation is a psychic act. It has a bearing on the whole problem of the artist's relation to inner and outer reality. If the act of destruction and breaking-up is primarily a mental act, and perceived as such, it is felt to be reparable in psychic reality. If a real person was broken up as Picasso breaks up his figures, it would certainly not be reparable in reality. But psychic reality is also very real; and the artist has a constant struggle against the anxiety about the final outcome of his endeavour. For example, if there is a rebellion against established canons, the artist has the anxiety about the effectiveness and worth of what he puts in their place.

This raises the whole problem of the artist's relation to reality. In popular myth an artist is a dreamer who ignores realities. And this is partly true – he may, for instance, ignore mundane realities of various kinds – but in a very important way the artist's relation to reality has to be very highly developed.

Freud compared the artist to a day-dreamer. And it is true that the poet is a day-dreamer; but he is not only a dreamer. Freud emphasizes that the artist returns to reality. I think the artist never quite leaves reality. To begin with, he has an acute awareness of his internal realities, the inner reality he seeks to express; but a grasp of inner reality always goes with the ability to differentiate what is internal and what is external and therefore also a sense of external reality – a basic difference between creativity and delusion. The artist must have an outstanding reality perception of the potential and of the limitations of his medium, limitations which he both uses and tries to overcome. He is not only a dreamer but a supreme artisan. An artisan may not be an artist, but an artist must be an artisan. And he is usually acutely aware of it.

In an interview (The *Guardian*, 12 November 1988), Arnold Wesker, speaking of the work of the writer, said:

> But I think there are two things needed to make anything universal: one is what you have selected; the metaphor you have chosen; and the other is the power of your perceptions of that metaphor, on that material. And if your perceptions are startling or vivid then they will carry over.

I would put it as follows: one is the creation of the symbol, and the other, the reality sense of the material means by which you express it.

There is another way in which the artist is related to reality. Achieving something in the external world is essential to his feeling of a completed reparation. Freud was right that in a sense the artist also returns to reality. He returns to external reality by doing something in and for the real external world. The crucial achievement in overcoming the depressive position is the infant's acceptance of his mother and other significant figures as really external and having an existence independent of himself. It is a crucial aspect of reparation as well as growing reality-sense that the child gradually relinquishes his phantasies of omnipotent control and in his mind accepts mother's independent existence, including her relationship with father, pregnancies with other babies and all extensions and symbolizations of these activities. So, if my assumption is correct – that the artist in his work is again working through his infantile depressive position – then he too has not only to recreate something in his inner world corresponding to the recreation of his internal objects and world, he also has to externalize it to give it life in the external world.

Some artists feel particularly strongly that the work acquires almost an independent existence. For instance, they create characters and feel they do not know which way those characters will develop. If that is missing, and one feels the author's hand too much in the characters, the reader has a feeling that the characters have been manipulated in a way going against their nature. The need to produce finally a work of art, which has to be produced in the external world and from which one has to be separated, often causes great anguish. I have seen in creative patients inhibitions in various stages of this process. Some have a difficulty in starting at all, and losing an idealized internal product; some have great difficulty in completing. So long as the work is not finished it is still their own. Some painters are well known for their reluctance to sell their pictures. They do not mind finishing so long as they continue to own them. Together with the achievement and the triumph of finishing, there is always a very painful process of separation. An important aspect of reparation is to let the object go. And another reparative aspect is of course the artist's gift of his work to the world.

A patient of mine conveyed very vividly the relation that has to be established between the internal and the external. He was struggling with a piece of writing – I think basically with overcoming megalomanic and narcissistic trends in his personality which were holding up his work. He described meeting on Hampstead Heath a writer who was walking along, looking at his shoes. He thought of him with approval, saying that he liked people walking that way because it meant they were concerned with their own thoughts. However, he praised this writer for a particularly vivid description of the Heath and its history. And I pointed out to him that the writer could hardly have done that if he always looked at his own shoes only. And then my patient had a vivid perception of a process, thinking he must look out and perceive; then he must look in at what he makes of it; and then he must do something 'out there', talking to his readers.

Throughout this chapter, I have emphasized how the creative impulse arises out of depressive anxieties, and how their expression in a way meaningful to the recipient involves such processes as are mobilized in the depressive position: the capacity to symbolize; perception of inner and outer reality, and ability to bear eventual separation and separateness.

Excessive defences against a set of feelings characterizing the depressive position can inhibit artistic creativity or they can be reflected in the final product. Schizoid and manic defences based on denials of psychic realities mar the aesthetic experience. Rodin expresses it better than I can. Contrasting what is ugly in nature and in art, he says:

Ugly in art is all that is false, artificial, that which aims at being pretty or beautiful instead of expressive. That which is mawkish, precious ... all that is parody of beauty or grace, all that lies.... When an artist, to add beauty to nature, adds more green to the Spring, more rose to dawn, more cadmium to young lips, he creates ugliness because he lies.

For an artist worthy of his name all is beautiful in nature because if his eyes accept without flinching all external reality – it reflects without fail like an open book all internal truth.

To Rodin all artistic beauty lies in facing true perceptions, external and internal, and all aesthetic failure in denial of internal truth. To me it sounds like the description of the perception gained in facing the depressive position.

I emphasize throughout the impetus for artistic creativity in the reparative impulses of the depressive position. But that necessitates an integration and a working through of earlier mental states, and integration of the perception of chaos and persecution, and that of an ideal state lost at the inception of integration. There is a longing to recreate an ideal state of mind and objects before what is felt as the havoc of the depressive position. Often the search is to regain a lost and unattainable ideal. Baudelaire writes: 'Mais le vert paradis des amours enfantines,/ L'innocent paradis, plein de plaisirs furtifs / Est-il déjà plus loin que l'Inde ou que la Chine?' (*But is the green Paradise of infantile loves, the innocent paradise, full of furtive pleasures, further now than India or China?*)

In *Invitation in Art* Adrian Stokes makes the, to me, very convincing point that part of the difficulty in art is that it is to satisfy both the longing for an ideal object and a self merged with it, with the need to restore a whole object realistically perceived, a separate mother not merged with the self. He suggests that the particular feeling of being drawn into and enveloped in a work of art has elements of the original pre-depressive merging with the ideal object. But the artist also has to emerge from it to be creative at all. This process is beautifully conveyed in Richard Holmes's *Footsteps*, in which he describes how he came to be a biographer. At the age of eighteen he decided to follow the footsteps of Robert Louis Stevenson recorded in *Travels with a Donkey in the Cévennes*. Step by step, he followed Stevenson's trajectory, trying to reconstruct both his hero's actual adventures and his state of mind. One day he came to the old Bridge of Langogne, which Stevenson had crossed, and found it was broken, crumbling, and covered with ivy. There was no way of crossing it. He had to cross on a modern bridge. 'The discovery put me in the blackest gloom.' In the night he had a dream from which he woke with new thoughts.

It was important for me because it was probably the first time that I caught an inkling of what a process (indeed an entire vocation) called 'biography' really means. I had never thought about it before. 'Biography' meant a book about someone's life. Only, for me, it was to become a kind of pursuit, a tracking of the physical trail of someone's path through the past, a following of footsteps. You would never catch them; no, you would never quite catch them. But maybe, if you were lucky, you might write about the pursuit of that fleeting figure in such a way as to bring it alive in the present.

Those were his thoughts at eighteen. Later he describes the process of writing a biography as having two main stages. The first stage is the living fictional relationship and a more or less conscious identification with the subject, a kind of hero worship, a love-affair, but one which includes a deep identification, a form of identification which he also calls a 'self-projection' (projective identification?). This he says is in a sense a pre-biographic, pre-literate state of mind, which is an essential motive for following in the footsteps.

But the true biographic process begins precisely at the moment, at the places, where this naïve form of love and identification breaks down. The moment of personal disillusion is the moment of impersonal, objective re-creation. For me, almost the earliest occasion was that bridge at Langogne, the old broken bridge that I could not cross, and the sudden physical sense that the past was indeed 'another country'.

The breakdown of idealization and identification is what induced in him the blackest gloom, but it was also the moment of creation. Holmes later speaks of another discovery, and that is that the single subject of biography is a chimera,

almost as much as the Noble Savage of Jean-Jacques Rousseau, living in splendid asocial isolation. The truth is almost the reverse: that Stevenson existed very largely in, and through, his contact with other people.... It is in this sense that all real biographical evidence is 'third party' evidence; evidence that is witnessed.

Holmes also says:

In this way the biographer is continually being excluded from, or thrown out of, the fictional rapport he has established with his subject. He is like the news reporter who is told something in confidence, 'off the record', and then can do nothing about it until he has found independent evidence from other sources. His lips are sealed, his hands tied. Otherwise he is dishonourable and prosecutable, not only in the courts of Justice, but in the courts of Truth as well.

In those passages Holmes compresses two important aspects of the depressive position. One is 'the evidence', the objective assessment of the situation – as in the dream of my Patient K (Chapter 4), where she observes the couple in the glade. This capacity to observe can precede the triangular situation. It is a real knowledge of the object with its good and bad aspects, a reality-testing which is an achievement of the depressive position. Wordsworth calls it 'emotion recollected in tranquillity'. The other is the statement Holmes makes that the biographer is continually being excluded from the fictional rapport he has established with his subject and that no one exists in isolation, but only in and through contact with other people. Hence the necessity of recognizing the triangular situation. Another discovery of the depressive position is that one cannot restore a mother without restoring the whole family she is related to.

Holmes's whole book describes to me very vividly both the schizoid search for the ideal object with whom one identifies and merges, and the depressive pain the artist has to go through to renounce it in order to achieve truth. And in the description he seems to convey the sense of the need of separateness, the acceptance of the triangular situation from which one is excluded and the need to bring to life again not just the beloved object, but the whole world that object is related to. This is biography as art. And it is not surprising that Holmes's biography of Shelley is generally acknowledged as a masterpiece. He also makes the point in his book that at best biography is an imaginative recreation, but one that must be as close as possible to what might have been the actual truth.

Biography of course is in many ways different from a purely imaginative work of art. Yet it seems to me that the elements he describes are the same as are true of all creative work: an unceasing search to reconstruct 'inevitable truths' and to find means of symbolizing them in a way that impels us to relive and continue further that search.

100

8

Imagination, play and art

Unconscious phantasy underlies and colours all our activities however realistic. But certain phenomena and activities aim more directly at the expression, elaboration, and symbolization of unconscious phantasies. Not only night dreams, but also day-dreams, play, and art, fall under this heading. They have many elements in common. Freud showed the closeness between day-dream and dream, and day-dream and art. Klein at times compared play with free associations and dreams, and emphasized the crucial role of play in the whole development of the child, including sublimation, and considered inhibitions in play as a most serious symptom. Art and play, however, differ from dream and day-dream because, unlike those, they are also an attempt at translating phantasy into reality.

Play is a way both of exploring reality and of mastering it; it is a way of learning the potential of the material played with, and of its limitations, and also the child's own capabilities and limitations. It is also learning to distinguish between the symbolic and the real. The child is aware that to play is to 'pretend'. The little child who makes pies out of sand sometimes tries to eat them or feed them to others. But it soon learns that pies made of sand are not for eating or feeding: they are 'make-believe' pies. In the normal child this will not inhibit his play. He will enjoy the satisfaction of expressing his phantasy of being mother or father cook, and the pleasure of having in reality made a new, attractive object. His play can then become increasingly imaginative: exploring what else can be done with, and be represented by the sand, sand which is not in fact a pie and which therefore can be used in many different ways.

A child's normal play is a major way of working through a conflict. I remember watching a boy of just under three, when his mother was away for a day giving birth to his first sibling. First he made a complex rail track for his wooden toy train. He filled it with little toy people and they had several crashes. Then he brought in ambulances. Soon he delineated some fields with his little bricks and filled them with toy animals. A complicated play resulted in shifting male, female, and baby animals in and out of the fields and train. There were fights and crashes; ambulances came to the rescue. Throughout, he was telling himself stories. He introduced bigger toy men to regulate the traffic, and so on. In other words, he represented the birth of new babies and his conflicts about it in very many different ways. For an interested observer it was fascinating to watch.

The capacity to play freely depends on the capacity for symbolization. When the symbolic function is disturbed it may lead to inhibition. In the case of an autistic child the inhibition is almost total. A disturbance of symbolization can also lead to forms of play which preclude learning by experience and freedom to vary play. When symbolization is dominated by primitive projective identification and the toy is symbolically equated too concretely with the object symbolized, it cannot be used imaginatively.

The little psychotic girl described by Geissman (1990) could, to begin with, only 'play' with pebbles. The 'play' was restricted to sucking them, spitting them out, or using them as weapons. Geissman-Chambon describes the evolution of the child's capacity to play with objects and to draw. Dick (Klein 1930), like that little girl, had an interest in only a few objects, particularly door-handles. In his material one can see that objects which for other children could be play material are too terrifying, too identified with phantasy persecutors, to be suitable for pleasurable play.

Play has roots in common with those of the night dream. Playing, like dreaming, is a way of working through an unconscious phantasy and it is subject to similar disturbances. The contrast between the play of the little boy described above and that of autistic children corresponds to the contrast I describe between the neurotic and psychotic use of dreams. Children who are not psychotic may express their psychotic phantasies in play, thereby mastering them and subjecting them to reality-testing. But the boundaries between psychotic and neurotic are fluid; often the psychotic content breaks through the play.

For instance, a little girl of two and a half, at the beginning of her analysis, would get into a complete panic if, rummaging in her toy drawer, she came across a little toy lion. A small boy who used a little red car to represent himself one day accidentally broke the car. He became terrified, tried to hide under the analyst's skirt, clinging to her legs, shivering. It seemed that the car was felt to *be* him at that moment, rather than to *represent* him, and the breakdown of the little car was experienced as himself breaking down.

Play in such circumstances can become a life-and-death matter.

Obsessional defences against such psychotic fears may lead to rigidity in play, close to obsessional ceremonials. When psychotic content breaks through, play may have to be abandoned. Or when excessive defences against such anxieties are used it may become compulsive, rigid, and repetitive.

Like dreams, play is not primarily meant for communication; though, unlike dreams, it often becomes so. It is often a link between children playing together. In a psychoanalytic session, play, like dreams, quickly becomes a major means of communication. There is, however, an important difference between night dreams and play: it is a difference in relation to reality.

Night dream, the 'royal road', is concerned only with achieving a phantasy resolution to a phantasy problem: 'It's only a dream.' Not so play, which makes an important connection with reality. In Klein's view, children's play is a most important way of making a symbolic connection between phantasy and reality; and playing together is an important step in socialization. Two cannot dream together, but two or more can play together.

Day-dreaming is probably the activity closest to Freud's original idea of a libidinal wish-fulfilment. It largely ignores reality. In a day-dream one can be a hero, an accomplished lover, a genius, or whatever one chooses. Aggressive phantasies can find their fulfilment, in being a great warrior, commanding armies, leading brigands, and so on – though usually the day-dreamer wants to see himself as good too. Commonly, the robber would be a Robin Hood kind of hero. Day-dreaming always involves splitting. Unlike the night dream, the day-dream ignores internal reality and deeper conflict. It is an omnipotent wish-fulfilment. It is indeed much closer to the original 'wish-fulfilment' as described by Freud than the night dream. Therefore it is often repetitive and shallow, and always egocentric. Characters other than oneself in the day-dream are usually cardboard ones. This kind of naïve day-dreaming is characteristic of latency and early adolescence. But adults day-dream too. It is only the most defended, restricted, and rigid individual who is bereft of day-dreams. Lack of day-dreams makes a very poor and dull personality. And one may well suspect that the unconscious phantasy is too horrifying to be allowed any access to the waking life and a day-dream. Our day-dreams often include our plans for the future, but in a more normal adult they are then subjected to reality-testing and abandoned or modified if they conflict with reality. However, day-dreams which continue unabated and intense into adulthood, and play an important role in mental life are usually a hallmark of schizoid borderline states, if not of psychosis.

A patient of mine, subject to psychotic breakdowns, when not in a state of breakdown spends hours fantasying in this way. He imagines himself as a great politician, or writer, or sometimes a Mafia leader, an only slightly updated version of his early-puberty day-dreams. His other 'day-dreams' are more overtly sexual. But even if they are not overtly sexual, when he is day-dreaming he is in a masturbatory state of mind, completely cut off from reality. This leads to a permanent vicious circle: the more he day-dreams the less he achieves in reality; and the less he achieves the more he is driven into his day-dreams. At times of acute stress the day-dreams take over, become his reality, and the outcome is a psychotic breakdown.

Day-dreams of this kind are very defensive and based on severe splitting in which reality perceptions and unwanted parts of the personality have been completely split off. Projective identification plays a large part: in latency and adolescence, various heroes are identified with. In more pathological day-dreaming projective identification may completely take over the subject's personality. A person living his day-dream is not, in fact, himself.

Day-dreams, understandably, have a bad press in psychoanalysis. And yet they are not far from something highly valued, that is, imagination. Day-dreams can be the beginning of story-telling. A patient of mine was very preoccupied in latency with day-dreams of the Robin Hood kind, but he would also tell stories based on these day-dreams to entertain his siblings and at times they became quite imaginative. It could have led to his becoming a writer. When Proust's Elstir, the painter, says, 'If a little dream is dangerous the cure for it is not less dreaming but more dreaming, the whole dream', he speaks not of night dreams but of day-dreams. It is his response to the narrator saying that his family complained of his spending too much time day-dreaming. I like to think that Elstir's 'more dreaming', 'the whole dream', refers to the move from day-dreaming to imagination. The whole dream, to my mind, means less splitting, more integration, and reaching deeper layers of the mind.

Freud has said that the artist's phantasy must lose its egocentric character to become compatible with art. 'Losing the egocentric character', I think involves a modification of the pleasure principle. It necessitates integrating one's perceptions of external reality that includes others and the perception of one's own relation to them. It also includes perception of the relations between them. In other words, imagination, unlike the typical day-dream, necessitates some abandonment of omnipotence and some facing of the depressive position. This makes imagination richer and more complex than a wish-fulfilling day-dream. The deeper the layers of the mind which can thus be mobilized, the richer, denser, and more flexible is imagination.

I shall illustrate the kind of shift between day-dreaming and imagination I have in mind by the material of a patient, L. L tends to get lost in a dream state in which the analyst, representing his mother, becomes erotized. As a child he oscillated between states of great over-activity and dreamy withdrawal. During the week preceding a holiday he was very inaccessible, but very comfortable and dreamy on the couch. Towards the end of the week he brought the following dream. *He was arranging some pink serviettes on a table and a woman disturbed him. He was absolutely furious and woke up with the strength of his fury.*

He associated the pink serviettes with an au pair he found attractive, and also with the 'pink brothels' which we had talked about before a previous holiday. (On that occasion he dreamed several versions of rooms with pink wallpaper which he associated to luxury brothels and to which we referred later as 'pink brothels'. They represented a phantasy of his being inside a very erotized maternal womb. At that time he was often in the daytime in a kind of dreamy, erotic haze.) He thought the woman in the dream who kept interrupting him must be the analyst interpreting. Suddenly he shifted to an apparently quite different theme. He said he went to see a Hogarth exhibition and was tremendously impressed. He liked Hogarth and had a book of photographic reproductions. But the reproductions were very different from the original lithographs. They were blurred, made smaller, and because they were photographs they were reversed – so different from the lithographs, which were precise, very deeply etched and gave an impression of depth. Knowing that he could well afford to buy what he pleased, I asked him, if the photographic reproductions were so unsatisfactory, why he bought them rather than some lithographs.

He laughed, and said I would find it hard to believe but he was very attracted by the fact that the pictures in the book were reversed. And then he added, 'I rather feel now like the adolescent I told you about who was completely mad and terribly proud of it. I thought the reverse pictures were something rather original and exciting.' He said that looking at the lithographs, he was also impressed to rediscover that they had a perspective and that they were very deeply etched, a feature not conveyed at all by the photographic reproduction. He then went on to say how much he admired Hogarth. Hogarth had such a precise vision. He could express fun, humour, sexuality, but never shirk the perception of degradation or horror as well. And he repeated, 'It is all so deeply etched.'

I think that in these associations he was showing the difference between a wish-fulfilling day-dream based on splitting, reversal,

105

idealization, self-idealization and complete egocentricity, his object being a pink brothel, de-humanized and only there to serve his needs, and Hogarth's imagination that is based on perception of reality which has perspective and which is 'deeply etched'. But at the moment when his associations shifted he was also showing a shift in himself from a masturbatory, day-dreaming state to one of feeling and imagination, since his own imagination was functioning when he was describing his reaction to the lithographs.

The next day he had a dream of *waiting for an elevator*. (He had lived for some time in the USA and occasionally used American expressions.) He did not associate directly to the dream but spoke with some pain and envy of a man, X, whom he had met the previous day. He had always been envious of X, whom he considered more intelligent and productive than he was himself. He remembered that some time ago X invited him to dinner and he could not go because his wife was ill. He, the patient, was furious with his wife, and he thought X would be annoyed with them too. But when he telephoned X he was surprised that X was very concerned about his wife's illness and asked him a lot about it. The patient was ashamed that he himself was so little interested in his wife's illness that he could not even adequately answer the concerned questions of his friend. He said he now realized that X functioned on some level quite different from that on which he himself functioned at the time. At that point I drew his attention to the fact that, unusually for him, he had called the lift an 'elevator', and suggested that his taking the elevator represented maybe his own wish to function on a more elevated level. He agreed with that, and added that there was a lift to the consulting-room which he never took. He always walked the two flights of stairs. Also, he wondered whether in the dream he wanted to wait for the lift because, when he walked up the stairs, he was usually alone on the staircase, and he thought of the lift as shared. I thought of the previous session and agreed that the higher level of mental functioning he was talking about involved the existence of others. I think his day-dream was losing its 'egocentric character' and coming closer to imagination. The 'higher level' involved admission of his rivalries and jealousy – for instance, of X. It also involved the recognition of pain in himself and in others, including a capacity for concern shown by the admired and envied X. In other words, it involved facing the conflicts of the depressive position. All those feelings were missing in his dreams of pink brothels and associated day-dreams, in which, paradoxically, he always saw himself alone.

I mentioned the patient who told stories to his siblings as one who might have become a writer. His analysis revealed why he could not become one; and indeed he never thought of writing as a possible profession for himself. He was a very defended, well-organized person, who sought treatment partly because of incomprehensible attacks of anxiety and depression. He always came to his sessions with 'a good story', not boring, nor necessarily shallow or repetitive, but always logical and consistent. Psychoanalytical insight itself was often used to make a connected coherent story about himself and others. Gradually a deep split was revealed. Behind the stories there was a feeling of chaos and dread – a horror which, unlike Hogarth, he could never integrate enough to be able to express and symbolize. His stories were still a defensive structure against a deeper and more anxious reality, just like the stories he told himself and his siblings to ward off nightmares.

It occurred to me, when reading science fiction, that the difference between day-dream and imagination could be seen as a difference between 'as-if' and 'what-if'. The bulk of pulp science fiction, known also as space opera, is an 'as-if' world: a martial hero or heroine conquers stars, roams space, and defeats villains. This kind of science fiction is pure escapism, making even day-dreaming easy, since someone else has made the effort to plot it. But not all science fiction is like that. There are science-fiction stories squarely rooted in reality. They are usually based on 'what-if': imagining what would happen if some parameter were changed, stories of what the future would be like if such-and-such were changed, like observing a certain social trend and projecting it into the future – 'what-if this trend prevails?' And not necessarily in the future: 'What would the world be like if such-and-such had happened in history instead of such-and-such?' Or, 'What if there was no gravity?' This kind of imagination does not deny reality to produce an 'as-if' world, but explores possibilities. Possible worlds are created through altering some factors to see 'what-if' and moulding the world into a new fantasy world with its own internal consistency and truth. I have of course oversimplified the problem, speaking of the themes of those stories. Content is not the only criterion: boy meets girl, boy loses girl, boy regains girl are the themes of much great literature. So can be the theme hero beats villain. There is always the question of form, style, depth of character, and all the other features which go into creating not an 'as-if' world but a psychologically true world, rooted in inner and outer truths. That applies to science fiction as to all forms of art. The difference between fantasy and imagination is the degree of denial of reality (Lepschy 1986).

In the *Two Principles of Mental Functioning*, Freud speaks of 'experimental thought':

A new function was now allotted to motor discharge which under the dominance of the pleasure principle had served as a means of unburdening the mental apparatus of accretions of stimuli.... Motor discharge was now employed in the appropriate alteration of reality. It was converted into action.

Restraint upon motor discharge (upon action) which then became necessary was provided by means of the process of thinking, which developed from the presentation of ideas.... It is essentially an experimental kind of acting accompanied by displacement of relatively small quantities of cathexis, together with less expenditure (discharge) of them.

(Freud 1911: 221)

Thought is a 'trial action'. Between desire and satisfaction there is a gap. Under the aegis of the pleasure–pain principle this gap is filled by hallucination – the world of 'as if'. The motor discharge which Freud sees in only energic terms, as a discharge of tension, I would see as a phantasied discharge of beta elements as well – a primitive process of projective identification.

When some reality is experienced I would see this gap as filled with a phantasy not omnipotently adhered to but open to testing. It can be tested in action – 'If I cry mother will come to feed me,' or 'If I defecate my hunger, it doesn't work; I am still hungry.' But phantasies are tested not only in action, or by perception of external reality only; they are also tested internally: 'If I kill my mother I suffer guilt and loss.' Such early phantasies are of a 'what-if?', not of an 'as-if' kind – they are 'experimental' phantasies, preverbal thoughts. They are the basis of rational action. Action is often rightly contrasted with imagination, but to be rational action must be based on imagination: foreseeing 'what will happen if I do this rather than that'. Play and art both need imagination, but play is primarily a child's activity. It often has a day-dream quality. Play may involve a minimum of imagination, or on the contrary may be very imaginative. It is also of course a beginning of work. It can involve frustration and pain, and necessitate perseverance. But by and large, if it stops being predominantly pleasurable it will be abandoned.

Not so art. Unlike play, artistic creativity involves much pain, and the need to create is compelling. It cannot easily be abandoned. Abandoning an artistic endeavour is felt as a failure, sometimes as a disaster. In creative work itself, whatever the joy of creating, there is also always an important element of pain as well. And it necessitates not only psychic work, which I spoke of in the preceding chapter, but also a vast amount of conscious work coupled with a high degree of self-criticism, often very painful. Artistic creativity has a lot in common with play, but is anything but 'child's play'.

Also, play is only incidentally a communication, whereas art is not only an internal communication. It is a communication with others. And much of the work consists of creating new means of communication. The little boy's play I describe at the beginning of this chapter was fascinating to an interested observer, but to an interested observer only. The artist's work must change his audience into interested observers. The artist must arouse an interest and make an impact on his audience. Finding new symbolic means of doing so is the essence of his work. Children's drawings, modelling, writing are steps between play and art.

Day-dreaming, dreaming, play, and art are ways of expressing and working through unconscious phantasy and are subject to similar disturbances. But what is the difference between them? The understanding of the night dream is the 'royal road' to the unconscious; reality-testing and reality activity are suspended and the working-through occurs in symbolic mental representation only. The day-dream is more defensive. It is rationalized and made acceptable to the waking ego. It is based predominantly on splitting and denial, and belongs mostly to schizoid functioning. But as I have tried to show, in a normal individual day-dreams persist, even when splitting is diminished, and they can evolve and become imagination, which is the basis of both play and art. Play is more than a day-dream. In normal play various aspects of life and its conflicts can be expressed. Unlike a day-dream, it also takes account of the reality of the materials played with, and is thus a process of learning and mastering reality. Art in that way is closer to play than to a dream or a day-dream, but it is more than play alone.

All children, except the illest, and all adults, play; few become artists. Neither dream, day-dream, nor play involve the work, both unconscious and conscious, that art demands. The artist needs a very special capacity to face, and find expression for, the deepest conflicts, to translate dream into reality. He also achieves a lasting reparation in reality as well as in phantasy. The work of art is a lasting gift to the world, one which survives the artist.

Bibliography

Arnheim, Rudolf (1962) *Picasso's* Guernica *Genesis of a Painting*, Berkeley: University of California Press.

Baudelaire, C.P. (1857) 'Moesta et errabunda', 'Spleen et idéal', *Fleurs du Mal*, 62.

Bell, C. (1914) *Art*, Oxford: Oxford University Press, 1987.

Bion, W.R. (1957) 'Differentiation of the psychotic from the non-psychotic personalities', *International Journal of Psycho-Analysis*, 38. Also in *Second Thoughts*, W.R. Bion, London: Heinemann, 1967.

—— (1958) 'On hallucination', *International Journal of Psycho-Analysis*, 39.

—— (1961) *Experiences in Groups*, London: Tavistock.

—— (1962) *Learning from Experience*, London: Heinemann.

—— (1963) *Elements of Psychoanalysis*, London: Heinemann.

—— (1965) *Transformations*, London: Heinemann.

—— (1970) 'Attention and Interpretation', in *Seven Servants: Four works by Wilfred R Bion*, New York: Aronson, 1977.

Britton, R. (1989) 'The missing link: parental sexuality in the Oedipus complex', in *The Oedipus Complex* by R. Britton, M. Feldman, and E. O'Shaughnessy (J. Steiner (ed.)), London: Karnac.

Conrad, J. (1897) *The Nigger of the 'Narcissus'*, in Conrad (1946-50).

—— (1902) *The Heart of Darkness*, in Conrad (1946-50).

—— (1903) *Typhoon* in Conrad (1946-50).

—— (1912a) *A Personal Record* (first published under the title *Some Reminiscences*), London: Dent (1916).

—— (1912b) 'The secret sharer', (a Tale in *Tales twixt Land & Sea*) in Conrad (1946-50).

—— (1917) 'The shadow-line', in Conrad (1946-50).

—— (1946-50) *The Collected Edition of the Works of Joseph Conrad*, London: Dent.

Ehrenzweig, A. (1948) 'Unconscious form creation in art', *British Journal of Medical Psychology*, 21.

Freud, S. (1900) *The Interpretation of Dreams, Standard Edition of the Complete*

Psychological Works of Sigmund Freud (SE) 4–5.

—— (1905a) 'Three essays on the theory of sexuality', SE 7.

—— (1905b) *Jokes and their Relation to the Unconscious*, SE 8.

—— (1907) 'Delusions and dreams in Jensen's *Gradiva*', SE 9.

—— (1908) 'Creative writers and day-dreaming', SE 9.

—— (1910) *Leonardo da Vinci and a memory of his childhood*, SE 11.

—— (1911) 'Formulations on the two principles of mental functioning', SE 12.

—— (1913) 'The theme of the three caskets', SE 12.

—— (1914a) *The Moses of Michelangelo*, SE 13.

—— (1914b) 'On narcissism: an introduction', SE 14.

—— (1914c) 'On the history of psycho-analytic movement', SE 14.

—— (1915a) 'Instincts and their vicissitudes', SE 14.

—— (1915b) 'The unconscious', SE 14.

—— (1916-17) *Introductory Lectures on Psychoanalysis*, SE 15-16.

—— (1920) *Beyond the Pleasure Principle*, SE 18.

—— (1923) *The Ego and the Id*, SE 19.

—— (1925a) 'An autobiographical study', SE 20.

—— (1925b) 'Negation', SE 19.

—— (1926) *Inhibitions, Symptoms and Anxiety'*, SE 20.

—— (1928) 'Dostoevsky and parricide', SE 21.

—— (1933) *New Introductory Lectures on Psycho-Analysis*, SE 22.

—— (1940) *An Outline of Psycho-Analysis*, SE 23.

—— (1950 [1887-1902]) *The Origins of Psycho-Analysis*, SE 1.

Fry, Roger (1924) *The Artist and Psychoanalysis*, London: Hogarth.

Geissman, Claudine (1990) 'L'Enfant aux billes: essais sur la communication chez un enfant autiste', *Journal de Psychanalyse de l'Enfant*, 8.

Goethe, J.W. (1832) *Faust*. Part 2, Act 1 (5). Finstere Galerie.

Golding, W. (1964) *The Spire*, London: Faber.

Heimann, P. (1950) 'On counter-transference', *International Journal of Psycho-Analysis*, 31.

Holmes, R. (1974) *Shelley: the Pursuit*, London: Weidenfeld & Nicolson.

—— (1985) *Footsteps*, London: Hodder & Stoughton.

Isaacs, S. (1948) 'The nature and function of phantasy', *International Journal of Psycho-Analysis*, 29; and in *Developments in Psycho-Analysis* M. Klein, P. Heimann, S. Isaacs, and J. Riviere (eds), London: Hogarth.

Jones, E. (1916) 'The theory of symbolism', *Papers on Psycho-Analysis*, London: Baillière, Tindall & Cox.

Kjetsaa, Geir (1988) *Fydor Dostoevsky*, London: Macmillan.

Klee, Paul (1908) *Journal 844*. Quoted in Robert Lyndon (1936) *Klee*, London: Spring Books.

Klein, M. (1923) 'The role of the school in libidinal development', in Klein (1975) *The Writings of Melanie Klein*, vol. I, *Love, Guilt and Reparation and*

111

other works 1921-45, London: Hogarth Press.

—— (1929) 'Infantile anxiety situations reflected in a work of art and the creative impulse', in Klein (1975, ibid.).

—— (1930) 'The importance of symbol-formation in the development of the ego', in Klein (1975, ibid.).

—— (1931) 'A contribution to the theory of intellectual inhibition', in Klein (1975, ibid.).

—— (1935) 'A contribution to the psychogenesis of manic-depressive states' in Klein (1975, ibid.).

—— (1940) 'Mourning and its relation to manic-depressive states', in Klein (1975, ibid.).

—— (1946) 'Notes on some schizoid mechanisms', in Klein (1975) *The Writings of Melanie Klein*, vol. III, *Envy and Gratitude and Other Works 1946-63*, London: Hogarth Press.

—— (1952) 'The mutual influences in the development of ego and id', in Klein (1975, ibid.).

—— (1975) *The Writings of Melanie Klein*, vol.I, *Love, Guilt and Reparation and Other Works 1921-45*; vol.II, *The Psycho-Analysis of Children*; vol.III, *Envy and Gratitude and Other Works 1946-63*; vol.IV, *Narrative of a Child Analysis*, London: Hogarth Press.

Lepschy, G. (1986) 'Fantasie e immaginazione', *Zeplettere Italiane*, NI – 39.

Lyndon, Robert (1936) *Klee*, London: Spring Books.

Meltzer, D. (1966) 'The relation of anal masturbation to projective identification', *International Journal of Psycho-Analysis*, 47; and in *Melanie Klein Today*, E. Bott Spillius (ed.) London: Routledge, 1989.

Money-Kyrle, R. (1965) 'Success and failure in mental maturation', in Money-Kyrle (1978).

—— (1968) 'On cognitive development', *International Journal of Psycho-Analysis*, 49; and in Money-Kyrle (1978).

—— (1978) *The Collected Papers of Roger Money-Kyrle*, Strath Tay: Clunie Press.

Mooney (1896) 'The ghost-dance religion and the Sioux outbreak of 1890', *Annual Report of the Bureau of American Ethnology*, 14 (2), Washington, DC.

Proust, Marcel *A la Recherche du Temps Perdu*, Harmondsworth: Penguin.

Rickman, J. (1940) 'On the nature of ugliness and the creative impulses', *International Journal of Psycho-Analysis*, 40.

Rilke, R.M. *Duineser Elegien* 1,4.

Rodin, A. (1911) *l'Art* (Dialogues with Paul Gsell), Paris: Gresset.

Rosenfeld, H. (1952) 'The psychoanalysis of the superego conflict in an acute schizophrenic patient', in *Psychotic States*, London: Hogarth Press.

—— (1962) 'The superego and the ego ideal', in *Psychotic States*, London: Hogarth Press.

—— (1964a) 'The psychopathology of narcissism' in *Psychotic States*, London:

Hogarth Press.

—— (1964b) 'An investigation into the need of neurotic and psychotic patients to act out', in *Psychotic States*, London: Hogarth Press.

Rothstein, Arnold (ed.) (1985) *Models of the Mind*, New York: International Universities Press.

Segal, H. (1950) 'Some aspects of the analysis of a schizophrenic', *International Journal of Psycho-Analysis*, 31; and in Segal (1986).

—— (1952) 'A psycho-analytic contribution to aesthetics', *International Journal of Psycho-Analysis*, 33; and in Segal 1986.

—— (1957) 'Notes on symbol formation', *International Journal of Psycho-Analysis*, 38; and in Segal (1986); and in Spillius (1989).

—— (1964) *Introduction to the Work of Melanie Klein*, London: Heinemann.

—— (1972) 'A delusional system as a defence against the emergence of a catastrophic situation', *International Journal of Psycho-Analysis*, 53.

—— (1978) 'On symbolism', *International Journal of Psycho-Analysis*, 59.

—— (1981) 'The function of dreams', in *Do I Dare Disturb the Universe?*, J.S. Grotstein (ed.), Beverly Hills, CA: Caeswa Press.

—— (1982) 'Early infantile development as reflected in the psychoanalytical process: steps in integration', *International Journal of Psycho-Analysis*, 63.

—— (1983) 'Some clinical implications of Melanie Klein's work', *International Journal of Psycho-Analysis*, 64.

—— (1985) 'The Klein-Bion Model', in *Models of the Mind* in Rothstein (1985).

—— (1986) *The Work of Hanna Segal*, London: Free Association Books.

—— (1989) *Klein*, London: Karnac.

Sharpe, E. (1930) 'Certain aspects of sublimation and delusion', *International Journal of Psycho-Analysis*, 11.

Shelley, P.B. (1812) Bodleian manuscripts, Folder 21–23. Also quoted in Holmes (1974).

—— (1821) *Epipsychidiom*.

Spillius, E.B. (1989) *Melanie Klein Today*, London: Routledge.

Stokes, A. (1965) *The Invitation in Art*, London: Tavistock.

Strachey, J. (1934) 'The nature of the therapeutic action of psycho-analysis', *International Journal of Psycho-Analysis*, 15.

—— (1958) Editor's note: 'Formulations on the two principles of mental functioning', *Standard Edition of the Complete Psychological Works of Sigmund Freud*, 12: 215.

White, P. (1970) *The Vivisector*, London: Cape.

Winnicott, D.W. (1971) *Playing and Reality*, London: Tavistock.

Wollheim, R. (1969) 'The mind and the mind's image of itself', *International Journal of Psycho-Analysis*, 50.

—— (1973) *Art and the Mind*, London: Allen Lane.

Wordsworth, W. (1850 [1805]) *The Prelude*, Book I.

Name index

Arnheim, R. 91–2

Baudelaire, C.P. 98
Bell, C. 1, 78–9, 80–2
Bion, W.R. x, 1, 49–50, 51, 57–8,
    64–5, 69
Britton, R. 58–9, 68

Cézanne, P. 86
Colette, S.G. 85, 86
Conrad, J. 88–9

Dostoevsky, F. 75
Duthy, C. 43

Ehrenzweig, A. 94
Ellis, H. 12

Ferenczi, S. 38
Freud, A. ix
Freud, S. x, xi, 1, 25, 29–30, 65,
    107–8; and art 74–84, 104; on
    dreams 3–4, 5, 12–14, 17–18; and
    instinct 19–20; on Michelangelo's
    Moses 82, 83, 89, 92; and phantasy
    16–18, 21, 30, 104; on symbolism
    12, 31–2
Fry, R. 1, 77–8, 79, 80–1, 94

Gautier, T. 81
Geissman, C. 35, 102
Goethe, J.W. von 93
Golding, W. 92
Goya y Lucientes, F. 80
Gsell, R. 82

Heimann, P. 12
Holmes, R. 98–100

Isaacs, S. 19, 20, 24

Jones, E. x, 32
Joseph, B. ix–xii

Kjär, R. 85–6
Klee, P. 93
Klein, M. ix, x, xi–xii, 1; on art and
    creativity 85, 86; and children's play
    101, 102, 103; and death instinct 21;
    on depressive and paranoid-schizoid
    positions 27, 35, 86; and narcissism
    25; and symbolism 33–4, 38; and
    unconscious phantasy 18–19, 20, 21,
    30

Lacan, J. 46
Langs, R. x
Leonardo da Vinci 74–5, 76
Lepschy, G. 107

Mallarmé, S. 81
Matthews, D. ix
Meltzer, D. 39
Michelangelo 79, 82, 83, 89
Money-Kyrle, R. 47–8, 56
Mooney, J. 37

Nietzsche, F. 93

Picasso, P. 80, 91, 94, 95
Piontelli, A. 69

114

Subject index

acting in xi, 26, 65, 69, 70
acting out 26, 68–9, 70, 72
adolescence: day-dreaming in 103; identification with heroes in 104; schizophrenia in 48
aesthetic experience/pleasure 77, 79, 81–3, 89–90, 94
aesthetics xi, 1, 74, 78, 79, 89
aggression 4, 8, 23, 40, 80; anxiety and guilt due to 33–4; art and 92–3
alpha elements 51, 53, 55–7, 61, 73
ambivalence 5, 41, 42, 61
analyst: ambivalence toward 41; containment by 61, 71, 72; death wish toward 14; idealization of 23, 29; identification with 26; in maternal role 8, 26, 39, 46, 105; in paternal role 41, 46, 47; phantasy about 5, 7, 59, 60; projection into 52, 53, 65, 67; understanding of 53, 61, 65
anxiety 7, 39, 53, 54, 103, 107; in childhood 85–6; and defence 21, 42, 103, 107; depressive 25, 42, 43, 56, 97; ego and 13, 20; and guilt 4–5, 33–4, 51; persecutory 85
anxiety dream 12, 14
art xi, 18, 80, 108, 109; and aggression 92–3; beauty and ugliness in 89–91, 94, 97–8; and depressive position 85–100; Freud and 74–84; phantasy and 75, 81, 89, 101, 104; significant form in 78, 80, 81, 89; symbolism and 33, 41, 43, 78, 81, 87
autism 34, 102

beta elements 51–3, 55–7, 61, 65, 73, 108
biography 98–100
borderline disorder 35, 54, 58, 65

castration fear 6, 33, 34
child analysis 18–19, 21–2, 34, 35–7, 43–6, 102
clinical material 5–6, 23–6, 34–5, 70–3, 97, 103–7; Patient A 29, 47, 94; Patient B 9–11, 14; Patient C 39–41, 47, 58, 59; Patient D 51–3, 61; Patient E 54–5; Patient F 60–1; Patient G 65, 68, 69, 72; Patient H 65, 68–9, 72; Patient K 59–60, 100; Patient L 105–6; Patient M 66–8, 72; Patient O 6–7, 21
communication 52, 64, 65; and play 103, 109; symbolic 39, 42
containment 50, 55, 57–8, 70; by analyst 61, 71, 72; identification and 51, 56; splitting and 53–4
creativity, artistic 18, 74, 75, 90; and day-dream 76–7, 95–6; inhibition of 97; perception and 96, 98; play and 77, 79, 108–9; reparation and 86, 89, 94–8, 109; symbolization and 86, 95

day-dream xi, 17, 101; artistic creativity and 76–7, 95–6; as defence 104, 109; dream and 3–4, 101, 109; and imagination 104–5, 106, 107, 109; and wish-fulfilment 103–5
death instinct 13, 14, 21

116

and working through of conflict 101
pleasure(–pain) principle 16–17, 76–7, 82, 104, 107–8
primary process 17
projection 8, 21, 24, 47, 49, 66; into analyst 52, 53, 65, 67; of beta elements 51, 52; as communication 65; as defence 21, 22, 29; in infancy 26–8, 38, 48, 50, 53–5, 58; and introjection 25, 70; of self 7, 26, 28, 34, 39, 67; symbolism and 38
projective identification 34, 42, 48–50, 56, 68, 108; and concretization 38, 39; and containment 57, 72; and day-dream 104; in infancy 26–8, 46, 50, 52, 57; pathological 49, 70; symbolization and 38, 102; withdrawal of 28, 40, 49
psychic conflict 13, 32, 48, 80, 89; unconscious 4, 33, 64, 74, 79; working through of 14, 79, 101
psychic work 94, 95, 108; dream-work and 12, 14–15, 33, 64
psychosis 42, 49; cases of 34–5, 53, 70–3, 103–4; child 35–7, 39, 102; dream, hallucination and 14, 34, 64, 65, 70; splitting in 52, 65

reality: artist's relation to 82, 89, 95–6; denial of 40, 81, 82, 97, 107; misperception of 68; perception of 29–30, 95, 97, 100, 101, 104; phantasy and 23–6, 28, 29, 101, 103; psychic 16, 40, 81–2, 89, 95–7; psychosis and 64, 65, 104
reality principle x, 17, 76, 82
reality-testing 20, 27–30, 56, 100, 103, 108
regression 3–4, 48, 49
reparation 14, 29, 41, 66, 85, 92; and artistic creativity 86, 89, 94–8, 109; and depressive position 28, 95, 98; and object loss 28, 38
repression 3–4, 12–13, 60, 70, 77, 79; as defence 25, 29; depressive position and 28–9; ego and 14, 15; phantasy and 17, 18, 31, 82; symbolization and 32, 33

sadism, sado-masochism 24, 61, 70, 80
schizoid state 29, 42, 103, 109
schizophrenia 24, 35, 42, 48, 58, 64
science fiction 107
secondary process 16
self: ideal object merged with 98; idealization of 23, 106; and object differentiation 28, 29; projection of 7, 26, 28, 34, 39, 67; splitting/fragmentation of 34, 50, 58
sexual intercourse 61, 66, 70, 90; parental 59, 60, 62
space 85; mental 49–63, 72; transitional 57; triangular 58, 59, 60, 62
splitting 23, 48, 61, 107; and containment 53–4; and day-dream 103–5, 109; as defence 21, 22, 29; of ego 42, 49, 65; of object 21, 28, 49, 58; of personality 49, 75, 104; phantasy and 17, 21, 76; in psychosis 52, 65; of self 58
sublimation 29, 39, 101; phantasy and 18, 35; symbolism and 32, 41
superego 4, 14, 24, 25, 50, 79
symbolic equation x, 35, 41–3, 65
symbolism xi, 28, 31–48; alpha elements and 56; and art 33, 41, 43, 78, 81, 87; dream and 5, 31–2, 48, 65; identification and 38; mental space and 49–63; sexual 40; and sublimation 32, 41; unconscious 31, 32, 33, 81; verbalization and 43
symbolization/symbol formation x, xi, 11–12, 15, 31, 35, 65, 70; affect, idea and 32; and artistic creativity 86, 95; and communication 42; concrete 36–8, 42–3, 48–9, 51, 55–6, 102; of death 75; in depressive position 38, 40, 43, 49, 51, 57; and ego 34, 42; inhibition of 34, 102; of mother's body 33; and mourning 40; and object loss 40, 42, 47; and paranoid-schizoid position 49; phantasy/unconscious phantasy and 31, 33, 41–2, 74, 101; and play 33, 102; projection/projective identification and 38, 102; and repression 32, 33